Live Beyond Monday: Lessons Beyond the Seminary

Copyright © Brandi L. Rojas
ISBN: 978-1-7373229-3-1
LOC: 2022909305

Publisher, Editor and Book Design: Fiery Beacon Publishing House, LLC
Fiery Beacon Consulting and Publishing Group

Graphics: FBPH Graphics Team, Dashona Smith

This work was produced in Greensboro, North Carolina, United States of America. All rights reserved under International Copyright Law.

The contents of this work are not necessarily the views of Fiery Beacon Publishing House, LLC nor any of its affiliates. No portion of this publication may be reproduced, stored in any electronic system, or transmitted in any form or by any means (electronic, mechanical, photocopy, recording or otherwise) without written permission from Brandi L. Rojas and Fiery Beacon Publishing House, LLC. All individual authors in this work own copyright to their chapter only. Brief quotations may be used in literary reviews. Unless otherwise noted, all scripture references have been presented from the New King James version or Amplified version of the bible. All definitions in this work have been presented by Google Dictionary(copyright.)

LIVE BEYOND

Monday

Lessons Beyond the Seminary

Compiled by

Pastor Brandi L. Rojas

Visionary Author

And Featuring:

Apostle Cherry Teal

Prophetess Donna Dandie

Apostle Mona Lisa McCorkle

Apostle Reveena Blair

Minister Shakirah Green

Table of Contents

The Introduction   7

1

(D)oubted, but (N)ever Aborted   9

By Pastor Brandi L. Rojas

2

Black Sheep   29

By Apostle Cherry Teal

3

The Lady Warrior   41

By Prophetess Donna Dandie

4

The Process of the Journey: I Was Graced for This   68

By Apostle Mona Lisa McCorkle

5

The Process   88

By Apostle Reveena Blair

6

When the Mic Drops: Truth Behind the Scenes   102

By Minister Shakirah Green

Prayer of Strength for the Vessel   127

Connect with FBPH, LLC

The Introduction

"I called you! I chose you! I make no mistakes!"

Many are called, but few are chosen, as is the case with us. Let us be honest: none of us asked for this and quite honestly, we ran from it. Yes, we loved God with our whole hearts, but there was something about the weight of the call that made us run, or at least try our very best to do so.

Through tears we have come, pressed through, and survived and arrived at this very point in our lives. It was through the hardest of places, that we discovered that we were really in this "thing" for the long haul, and that our yes was truly our YES to Him without restraint.

No, we are not perfect.

Yes, we have made mistakes!

No, we do not have a perfect past, but God is using it for His perfected will!

It is our prayer that as you read this, you will discover the path we have taken to receive the oil and anointing that God has entrusted us with. It is our prayer, that you will not find yourself fearful of saying yes to Him, but instead even more deeply discover that you are NOT ALONE, and that it is ALL going to work out for good!

Allow these words to strengthen you, push you and encourage you. We declare it be so in Jesus' name!

AMEN!

[a]Therefore I urge you, [b]brothers and sisters, by the mercies of God, to present your bodies [dedicating all of yourselves, set apart] as a living sacrifice, holy and well-pleasing to God, *which is* your rational (logical, intelligent) act of worship. 2 And do not be conformed to this world [any longer with its superficial values and customs], but be [c]transformed *and* progressively changed [as you mature spiritually] by the renewing of your mind [focusing on godly values and ethical attitudes], so that you may prove [for yourselves] what the will of God is, that which is good and acceptable and perfect [in His plan and purpose for you].

Romans 12:1-2

Author
Pastor Brandi L. Rojas

Pastor Brandi L. Rojas is a native of Greensboro, N.C. She serves with her Husband, Pastor Omar Rojas at Maximizing Life Family Worship Center in Greensboro, N.C. a vision God birthed through them in 2015. Rojas has been in Dance Ministry for twenty-six years and is a 2009 graduate of the School of Disciples taught under the late Bishop Otis Lockett, Sr. In 2013, she was named Sweetheart of the Triad, an award given based on community involvement. Pastor Rojas was licensed to preach the Gospel on February 27, 2011, and as a result DYmondFYre Global Ministries was born. Rojas was ordained as an Elder June 22, 2012 and was installed as Pastor with her Husband on January 27, 2013.

Since that time, she, and her Husband, also known as #TeamRojas, by God's mandate, have birthed several evangelistic causes. In January 2014 Rojas opened FYreDance Studios and Liturgical Arts Consulting which provides on-site instruction, virtual teaching, consultation services, choreography services and dance encounters. The following year a prayer walk initiative was created to bring the local churches and community together to work together and help lead the lost to Jesus Christ and empower the world through a vehicle called The Gatekeeper's Legacy; since that time she has also served as part of the planning and leadership committee for the National Day of Prayer for the City of Greensboro and currently serves as the youngest committee member, only African-American and only female on the core team.

In February 2016, Rojas launched out again to begin IgniteHerSoul International Women's Fellowship (formerly The Legacy Ladies Fellowship), an organization created to help women of God pray, push, and live the reality of what God has called them to. The CrossOver Resource Center was later birthed out of the mandate of Maximizing Life FWC, which works to provide solutions for life's transitions to the community. Rojas released her first book in June 2016 entitled **In the Face of Expected Failure** and her sophomore project, **Humpty Dumpty in Stilettos: The Great Exchange**, in November 2016. It was with the second book release Fiery Beacon Publishing House, LLC was launched, serving current and upcoming authors, playwrights, and poets. Since that time, she along with her FBPH Team have been able to help over ninety authors launch and pursue their literary dreams along with owning the first Author Incubator Hub, "The Ink Lab," giving literary creatives a safe place to think and CREATE. Humpty Dumpty in Stilettos was nominated for the National Literary Trailblazer of the Year Award in 2017 by the Indie Author Legacy Award in Baltimore, Maryland and in July 2017 she was noted as an International Best-Selling Author for her part in a collaborative effort called **Stories from the Pink Pulpit: Women in Ministry Speak**.

Pastor Rojas has added to her list a number of other literary works including:

Rehobeth Church Road: Suicide in the Pulpit
(September 2019)

When Legacy Arises from the Threshing Floor: A Collective of Trials and Tribulations Superseded by Undeniable Triumphs (November 2019)

Before You Hit 40: Forty-One Pivotal Life Nuggets
(January 2020)

Not With Your Legs Crossed: #SpiritualBirthingUncensored (September 2020)

My Pink Stilettos (October 2020)

When Legacy Arises from the Threshing Floor: A Collective of Trials and Tribulations Superseded by Undeniable Triumphs Volume 2

(November 2020)

The Mantle I Never Asked For (November 2020)

Not With Your Legs Crossed #SpiritualBirthingUncensored (June 2021)

Talitha Koum: Get Up Little Girl, Get Up! (October 2021)

Build it A-Gain! Confessions of the Nehemiah Generation (October 2021)

Live Beyond Monday: Lessons Beyond the Seminary (May 2022)

Church Girl, Club Girl, God's Girl! (May 2022)

and more!

In the Marketplace, Pastor Rojas is known for her progressive efforts through her travel company, Fiery Beacon Travel, and the international platform of Surge365. She currently serves as a Regional Builder with the company and has received multiple bonuses while doing so. Rojas also makes it a priority to share the reality and necessity of multiple streams of income which empowers the home, community, nation, and world. Pastor Rojas is grateful and humbled at how God continues to expand the entire vision, not just to the United States, but internationally as well.

Team Rojas are the proud parents of five children, three godchildren and a host of spiritual children. Pastor Brandi Rojas is a Worshiper, Servant, Praise Vessel, and Prayer Warrior, but most of all, she is a vessel who is on fire for God.

To Connect with Pastor Brandi Rojas:

Phone: 336.285.5794

Email: fbphinfo@fierybeaconpublishinghousellc.com

Website: www.fierybeaconpublishinghousellc.com

Facebook: www.facebook.com/FieryBeaconPHLLC

IgniteHerSoul International Women's Fellowship:

ignitehersouliwf@gmail.com

Maximizing Life Family Worship Center:

www.facebook.com/MaximizingLife

Instagram: @allthingsdymondfyre / @maxlifefwc

My Dedication

I dedicate this chapter to every biological and spiritual child God has given me the honor of birthing and leading in this world.

May this chapter fuel you to do great and mighty things for God's kingdom, knowing that the way has already been paved, just for you.

1

(D)oubted but (N)ever (A)borted

By Pastor Brandi L. Rojas

Seven — I was seven years old the day I accepted Jesus Christ as Lord and Savior. I do not remember being nervous or even "shaking in my boots," but I do remember planning for that day and waiting in expectation for those infamous words to escape from the lips of my then Pastor, Dr. Cardes H. Brown, Jr. at New Light Baptist Church in Greensboro, North Carolina,

"Is there one?"

The song began to play in the background, but that quickly went on mute as I stood up and walked to the front, ready to surrender my life to the Savior. Now some may say that there is no way that a child that young can understand what they are doing in that moment, but as a lay member and even a Pastor, I can also say that I have witnessed many adults say YES, never understanding the depth of their surrender. I did not understand the depth of my YES that day, but I knew that it was real - I felt it in the pit of my soul.

As the years progressed, I experienced so many changes in my life, from the igniting desire to serve on the usher board, sing in the choir, my mother going through breast cancer and surgery, and later, even the loss of my father. I can say now freely — that was the loss that broke me. We had his funeral service at church, in the very space that I cherished, but from that moment I could not see the altar without seeing his casket lying there. From this place, there I sat, still singing, still serving, wanting to die, a heartbroken daddy's girl. It was around the time that my father passed that the look of our youth department changed, and we were blessed with an amazing Youth Pastor named Jerry O. Wilson who now serves as a Senior Pastor in a separate region of North Carolina. I could not pinpoint with accuracy the reason then, but he had the ability to push me into places of complete discomfort, like a father pushing his daughter on a new bike without training wheels, and no matter how scary it sounded, I was willing to do it. This scary place for one included public speaking.

Believe it or not, it did not matter how many times I took the karaoke machine my mom gave me, plugged it up and preached to myself in the mirror, there was something about doing it in front of real people. I am laughing as I type it now - I even remember trying to do it when my mom and brother were not home, listening for the key to turn in the deadbolt lock of our front door so that I could toss the mic and act as if it never happened. Pastor Wilson came to me one day and asked me to do the Youth Highlight — a short Word to encourage the people. To get ready for the moment, my mother even took me to the bible bookstore so that I could find just the right book to share from. When I found it, I felt as if a light had illuminated it — one hundred topics for youth! I knew that this was the perfect book and that all my problems were solved! We got the book, and before we even made it home, I began diving in, looking for just the perfect Word.

The Sunday finally came, and I wish that I could remember the date that escapes me completely, however the memory of it remains fresh. I ascended the pulpit and it seemed as if the whole room went quiet. I began to speak, and within minutes people began standing up on their feet. My peripheral was on one thousand, as I tried to see how my Youth Pastor and Senior Pastor were responding. There stood my Youth Pastor Jerry Wilson, with a huge smile on his face, and on the other side, Dr. Cardes H. Brown, Jr. standing behind me with his arms folded and his signature move when someone was doing their "good preaching," rubbing the top of his head in disbelief. For me, I was just reading from the paper, but those five minutes laid a seed of power that shocked everyone, including me.

Time went on, and as I served and moved, my spirit began to shift, too. I had to be around sixteen or seventeen years old when my grandmother, on my mother's side, got sick. She had been battling various diagnoses in her body, but this was different as the doctor's released the word, amputation. When my mother told me, I was devastated as we all were, but I knew I had to get to my grandma, alone, and I had to take my faith with me. I got to the hospital and opened the door to see her sleeping. I can still remember the light bouncing off her shiny, silver hair as the Andy Griffith Show played in the background. I walked in slowly and made sure that the door did not slam behind me. Even more slowly I approached and stood at the foot of her bed, just looking. In a fleeting moment, I saw a light overcast on her leg, the one scheduled for amputation. I looked in amazement and disbelief and found myself thinking that maybe coming alone was not the best idea. I looked around for any explanation for why the light was there.

It was not the TV; this light was brighter than that.

There was no light coming from the ceiling.

There were no machines producing light, not like this.

Tears fell from my eyes as I realized that I had just encountered the presence of God. I left that hospital room without ever waking her, with tears streaming down my face, knowing that no matter what the outcome, she would be just fine. Like the little girl I was at seven years old, that Sunday

I woke up, seventeen years old and rushing to get to church. Now, let me be clear – I had NO intentions on even sharing what happened, but I guess as the seasoned saints, say,

"It was like FIRE shut up in my bones!"

So, church commenced and as always, there was time afforded for an altar call. After the completion, and while people were walking back to their seats, I walked straight to the pulpit, and asked for the microphone.

Maybe I should digress and say this – I was not raised by anyone in ministry. I did not have anyone to confirm what God was calling me into, but I knew what I saw, and I knew on the inside of me, that it was Him. So, there I stood, with a mic in my hand, fully ready to share what I encountered in the quiet of the moments that I had with my grandmother. As I spoke, I could tell that some were listening intently, while others were staring at me like I had gone crazy. At the conclusion of my "testimony," you could have heard a pin drop, followed by one in the pulpit thanking God for what I shared and proceeding to the next act of worship. I walked back to my seat with my eyes filled with tears. There was no way that I could explain away what happened in that room, and quite honestly, I had no desire to even try.

Regardless of my path and process, I knew God was calling me to something great. Again, I did not have anyone to tell me who I was going to be — all I knew was that I loved Jesus and whatever He wanted from me, I was more than willing to do. It had to be about one year later, when someone I worked with invited me to visit a church with her. I went, and enjoyed every second of it, as the people praised and worshiped God in a way that made me want to pursue Him even more deeply. It was this place that shifted me from my childhood church into an even deeper destiny. Make no mistake about it, I knew God used New Light Missionary Baptist Church to plant the seed, and this next place, Evangel Fellowship under Bishop Otis Lockett, Sr., He was about to water it.

I received my first car at fifteen years old. By the time I turned sixteen, it did not take long before I had a whole stereo system installed in it. I will never forget....

A 1989 Volkswagen Jetta, with a system in the trunk and a plate on the front of the car with a blue cross and my name in airbrush, Brandi, in cursive black lettering outlined in white.

The main "attraction" to my car though, was the songs I played, as I rolled up the road bumping Kirk Franklin and others like it was nobody's business! Before I knew it, I had joined this new place of worship called Evangel, and within a few months, had begun dancing for the Lord and even attended 5 A.M. prayer meetings (I was the youngest person in attendance.) Whenever there was a moment for the doors of the church to open, I wanted to be there, I needed to be there. Over time, and as life progressed, I found myself feeling the fire slip, you know, go away. I had mentors around me by this time, but oh how I wish I had someone closer, bloodline wise, to tell me to jump back in the fight and push again! By the time I turned thirty years old, I had been married for six years, had an amazing son (who is now eighteen years old) and was sitting in the middle of a divorce. I was heartbroken, lost, angry and confused, but despite my position God always let me know that He was there.

It had to be around the summer of 2009 or 2010 when I met my Aunt Angie. My mom was going to a celebration of life for one of my relatives on my father's side of the family and asked if I wanted to go. I was not too sure, since I did not have a close relationship with them, however, I agreed and went. As we sat in the pew, my mother began pointing different people out to me, one being my father's sister, Angela. I sat and watched as the funeral proceeded. Once it was over, as all normally do, the fellowship continued outside. There I stood with my mother as she waited for the family members to become more visible, until she instructed me to come with her. We walked over to the limo, and it was there that she introduced me (yes, I said introduced) to my

Aunt. She looked, her eyes got so wide, and her mouth opened as she said with that unmistakable Connecticut accent,

Oh my God, BRANDI!

She immediately told everyone to move over in the limo, made room for me and invited me in the car. I could not explain it, but at once I felt this sense of restoration that I still cannot put into words. She looked at me and said,

"I have not felt the presence of your father so close since he passed, as I do right now."

Tears welled up in my eyes, as I wept with a smile on my face. She continued, but this time proceeded this way:

"If your father Nathaniel were still here, he would want me to tell you that he is so proud of you. He would want me to tell you that he sees you. He would want me to tell you that he loves you so much and that you must keep going, keep trying, keep dancing!"

Tears flooded our eyes and the limo that day, as I told her that I had just closed my dance studio months before; all she could say was, "MY GOD." I began to share as much as I could, but more than anything we exchanged phone numbers and vowed to connect; we knew that was a God-ordained moment, and even until this day, we still reach out as you will read over these next few pages.

So, we fast-forward again — within two- and one-half years I found myself going from broken, lost, helpless depressed and divorced, to restored, whole, remarried, expecting, and doing well. (There is so much more to share here, but it will be in my next solo release, <u>Church Girl, Club Girl, God's Girl!</u>) It was within this timeframe that I left the church completely, ran back to the club and the world, and found myself right back and the feet of Jesus. It was by this point that I had also been licensed as a minister and ordained as an Elder in the Lord's Church. These above truths, in this moment, justify a flashback.

I am the granddaughter (on my father's side) of one, Nehemiah Troxler. I only met him once — and that was at my daddy's funeral. I remember this short, chocolate-complexioned man with a smile that screamed heaven! I remember him telling me who he was, and the embrace he gave me when I smiled back through tears. I remember him telling me before he left, that he would keep in contact with me and that he loved me. Sadly, life is life, and we never had those moments but a far greater one was on the horizon. When I was around twenty-one years old, I remember this urge to find my grandfather, and quite honestly, I should probably call it a mandate, as it was an idea that literally

BOOMED in my spirit. So, I looked, and by the time I found him, he was in the hospital. I found a phone number and called to hear a male voice answer, who I later identified to be one of my uncles, Gad Troxler. When I told him who I was, he paused then said,

"Brandi! Nathaniel's daughter! Nehemiah, it's Nathaniel's daughter! She wants to talk to you!"

Excitement filled my soul, for I knew I heard the Lord and was about to be reunited with my grandfather. The phone must have been placed to his ear because I could hear him breathing, but it was only long enough to hear him take his last breath. Sorrow filled my soul, as I moved into a place of failure for not finding him more quickly and, at that moment, feeling as if the mandate received was for nothing. I never got to know him, outside of that sharp-dressing, chocolate, heavenly smiling man, but wait, there's more.

It had to have been a month or so before I had spoken with my Aunt Angie. It was right after I had gotten married and was about to be ordained. When I shared with her what was about to happen in my life, she screamed in the phone,

"Niece, are you serious?!"

I confirmed, excited about her excitement, but not truly understanding the question she asked. It was then that she told me that my grandfather was an Elder, too. Tears filled my eyes as she released this next statement,

> **"When he died, I was heartbroken because I thought that his anointing died with him, but it didn't – it's with YOU."**

The tears that stayed imprisoned by my attempt to hold them in were finally free, as I breathed in and out, remembering that moment he was in the hospital, taking his last breath. That moment was not a loss, it was a moment of transfer, one of which I received simply because I loved God and always told Him that I wanted to do His will and was willing to be His vessel. It was then that I realized that God had chosen me and activated His call in me through this delayed but on time exchange. To this day, I still wonder what having his wisdom to navigate through ministry would have been like. I still wonder what it would be like to have someone in my bloodline wrap me up in their arms, reassure me that I can do this and that I am going to do well. I still wonder what my daddy would say, and how he would respond knowing that I picked up what may have been meant for him but was placed on me. I still have those moments where I look at the parents, the Pastors, and Leaders, anoint their children for this work, and wonder how that would feel. It is this place that fuels me to provide what I never had the opportunity to receive.

As of today, I have been in ministry eleven years, two months, and twelve days, and pastoring for over nine years. Within that time, I have seen and experienced so much, and so, it is my honor to share a few of those lessons with you now.

1. No doubt – this is for you!

If I had allowed myself to fall for the process of LIFE, I would have found myself not only telling God "no," but telling Him "no," forever. Hear me, life and even people said that I never deserved to be called His minister or even a pastor. Some looked at my process as a disqualification and even to this day roll their eyes at me every chance they get; I guess that's part of what happens when you pastor in a place who has witnessed your process publicly. At first, I would want to pursue the WHY, but have instead given it over to God. Do not be mad at me, I didn't choose me either, and if people have an issue with it, they will have to consult with the One who chose me, you, US.

2. Just, breathe.

There are so many things I have endured as a pastor, and believe me, some of those things shook my world. I know "church hurt," as a lay member, but it does not compare to "pastoral hurt," or even "clergy hurt," for that matter. I know what it is to only be tolerated because of connections that others want to get to, and they know they must go through you, "the least of them," to get it. I know what it is to wonder why you were not picked but it seems like everyone you introduced to one another are the only ones invited while you are left in the shadows. I know the feeling of just wishing that you could disappear, as you constantly show up for others who may never show up for you. I know the feeling — God knows, I do. It was in these moments that I had to breathe; it was the mechanism that God gave me to reset myself while still hearing Him.

3. Simply become who you are.

This saying was a plaque that stayed on a shelf in my office at our previous church location — "simply, become who you are." I remember paying $4 for it, but its words were always an echo in my soul. Just as I talked about "church hurt," I remember being reminded of it as well by one who came with a question:

"After all the church has done to you, why would you want to become a Pastor?"

My answer was simply, "because it was through that place, that I learned who I wanted to be and who I cannot be. I must show the world who the church really is. I must help others know, what a Kingdom Pastor is like." This charge came with many mistakes and many days of personal imbalance. I remember moments when I would stay up countless nights trying to prove to people that I was not "that Pastor," who cared nothing for them, not realizing that I could not take on the pain or faults of another leader and submit to the punishments distributed to me. It was here that I realized that becoming a pastor meant leaving "me" behind, and while some would not like it, becoming who God called me would help to set so many people free. It was in this place, that I am still realizing what God has invested in me. It is in this place, that I am still, simply, yet lovingly and forcefully, becoming, B.

So, for those reading this chapter, whether as new leader or one who has been in this call for years, it is my hope and my prayer that something has been shared to arrest your mind and stir your soul. It is my prayer that these words will act as a salve, promoting healing and recovery. It is not easy, but I promise, it will be worth it. Keep going!

Humbly Submitted,

"A Pastor who wanted to die, but God commanded to LIVE."

Author
+Apostle L. Cherry Teal

Apostle Cherry, a native of Winston-Salem, NC was reared in holiness at a young age. Though like most young people who knew God has a plan for their lives, they try to fit in even though she clearly stuck out. Cherry had to acknowledge at an early age that she epitomized the scripture found in I Peter 2:9. After accepting that God chose her to be different, she submitted to his purpose for her life and began to gain the knowledge needed to equip her to do the HIS will. In May 2013, Cherry preached her initial sermon under the leadership of Bishop Stephon Samuels.

Holding true to Ecclesiastes 9:10 which declares "Whatsoever thy hands findeth to do, do it with thy might; for there is no work, nor device, nor knowledge, nor wisdom, in the grave, whither thou goest.," Cherry diligently served in the capacity of Worship Leader, Administrative Assistant, Financial Officer and Assistant to the Pastor. Cherry's ability to shift the atmosphere under the power of the Holy Ghost is like none other. She boldly uses the authority given to her to command things to be so.

Apostle Teal has served under some awesome leaders, all of whom acknowledged and cultivated the call on her life. It is under the leadership of Bishop Gonnie T. Baldwin, of The Uncompromising Word of Truth Praise and Worship Center

(TUWT), where she was ordained as an Elder in the Lord's Church in July 2018.

For some time, the Lord had begun speaking to Cherry about birthing her own ministry. In January 2019, the Lord clearly instructed her to begin to get her affairs in order and prepare for the transition to come. On Sunday, February 3, 2019, after ministering the preached word entitled "You're just right for the job" during the morning service, the Lord led Bishop to speak publicly what God had spoken to Cherry privately. It was on that Sunday, the Teals were released to launch their ministry.

Apostle Cherry Teal is the visionary of Restored Faith Ministries, where its motto is "Restoring Your Faith Back to its Purpose." She is the proud daughter of the Late Stanley Giles and Margaret Giles. She is a graduate of Winston-Salem Forsyth County School System. She has a degree in Early Childhood and Human Services from Forsyth Technical Community College. Cherry's biggest joy is serving in the role for the past 18 years as the wife of Overseer Kenneth D. Teal better known to her as "My Dude!" To this union, they have three beautiful children.

Above all, she's Saved, Sanctified, and Filled with the Holy Ghost. Cherry's life continues to be a testament to the fact the not only if God's hand firmly placed on her life, but that she clearly does not look like what she has been through. One of the songs she ministers shares just a snippet of her testimony... God is indeed her Way-maker, Miracle Worker, Promise Keeper, and a Light in the Darkness... That is who he is to her.

My Dedication

My chapter is dedicated to the late Stanley Edward Giles, Jr. My father was my biggest supporter. Before his passing, he shared with me the following words:

"Daughter, keep singing and preaching that Word! I love to hear you sing and preach. You have come a long way; don't let nothing, or nobody stop you!"

Not many days from hearing these words, my father passed away.

I love you, Daddy!

Connect with Apostle Teal!

Facebook: www.facebook.com/cherryteal1973

www.facebook.com/SEGConferenceCenter

Email: ladyteal73@yahoo.com

Phone: (336) 721-5338

2

Black Sheep

By Apostle L. Cherry Teal

Born August 4th, 1973, to Margaret & Stanley Giles Jr., I was the oldest of three siblings. Being raised in a Catholic and Apostolic home was a complete mess; however, my father gave us a choice whether to go with my mom or listen to his church recite Hail Mary. It was strange. We would go from shouting and praising God to kneeling before we went to our seats. Once we were seated, we would make the sign of the cross on your chest. What a crazy world huh? That was an understatement.

Life was good. My father owned his own business, every Friday we were able to go shopping and still received our weekly allowance. Once we were of age, we got our first car, and my parents paid our insurance until that first accident.

I grew up with a father who was Catholic and a mother who was Apostolic. Can you say complete chaos? My Father over here talking about "Hail Mary full of grace" and my mom is talking about "repent the Lord is at hand." Can somebody get me out of this mess? I was just as confused as I could be until I went to church with my grandmother on that Saturday night and saw the mothers calling on God and speaking in tongues. Of course, I was still confused until she got me on that floor, and I began calling on the name of Jesus myself. I did not know she told me to get up because I was not ready.

There was still something missing for me. I would go to church week after week. It would be that time that one Mother of the church would speak over my life. She began to share with my mom that I was going to be somebody great in the Kingdom. She went on to tell her that I had an old soul. What in the world was this lady talking about? Get out of here! As much as I have seen in the Apostolic Church, I dare not want to carry anything, let alone a Bible.

It would always amaze me that I could never fit in with everyone else. My mother would send me to church with my grandmother. Lord forbid, I did not want to go. All I wanted to do was be free to play with my friends and enjoy life. Life, what was that, because Lord knows that I had to come home from school to do chores, cook, clean, help my mother study, and hear my dad moaning because of Crohn's disease. I can remember a time that my dad would say that he did not understand why we were going to that church making all that noise when it was not necessary. It did not take all that.

Yes, I tried to go and hang out with my friends however I never felt comfortable in doing so. This led me to be so withdrawn from others, not fully understanding that the Lord was calling to Ministry early. Unlike everyone else, I ran. I did everything that I thought I could do until I got pregnant and was brought before the church. My mom lost it and dared me not to say anything to anyone. We left the Ministry and never turned back. Oh, my goodness! What was I going to do now? Can you say LOST?

It was when I moved out, had my own encounter with God in the church parking lot. I was told that I began to speak in tongues, crying and laying prostrate on the gravel. This was the moment that I knew I experienced God for myself. It was a feeling that I could never explain. All I knew was I wanted everyone to experience what I felt.

The sun has always shined, and I thought these could be the best days of my life but why did it not ever feel like I could ever enjoy the sun? The sun shined so bright at times that it felt like it could blind you when you tried to look at it. That was my life. A life that looked bright, yet it was blocked by the radiant sun.

As I sat in the backyard with the sun glistening and the wind blowing, I could hear all my friends screaming and enjoying the excitement of life. They had not a care in the world. They played with sticks, balls, rope, and chalk, which was the only thing that they were concerned about. It made no difference what the day was like as long as outside was the focus of the evening. Nothing even mattered what happened all day because they knew that on Friday night, a party was going down at the Giles household.

My dad was always on the road. There were even times that he would get stuck in Canada due to the weather. This would put my mom in a frenzy. She could barely read or add. She dropped out of school in the sixth grade to take care of her siblings. There were even times that I had to go to her job to complete her timesheet due to her not being able to add her time or read it. This was my day-to-day life while my dad was out driving up and down the road. This was now my life. A life full of ups and downs, ins and outs. What was really going on?

I became so angry and bitter until I fought my way out of a lot of situations. It was so bad that when my family would come around, they would turn around and leave if I were not in the room. I became so withdrawn until I started doing things that I knew were wrong. Yet and still that still voice was telling me, "Cherry don't do that." Yep, I still done that and some.

I still could feel a tugging in my spirit, however, I needed to be released from so many things. Anger, frustration, bitterness, my father being ill, apartment burning down, losing everything, going to jail for stealing diapers for my son, getting pregnant by a man that was not my husband, having an abortion, not speaking to my sibling for years, getting married to a cheater, attempting suicide, having to move out of my home unexpectedly, utilizing Section 8, breaking up property, cussing people out just because, attending college, fighting because I felt like it, attempting to raise a boy child alone, messing around with someone in the church. Just an emotional wreck.

What do you do when you are just sick of it all? Give it to God sincerely. I tried it all my way and lost it all. I lost my identity and dignity trying to prove a point to others that could care less about me. All I knew was Mother Cherry told my parents that I was going to be someone in the kingdom. She never said when, however, it was going to happen. I had to finally give up my right to be right for his right. What was it going to cost me? How long was I going to self-sabotage? How long was I going to make excuses for everyone else? When was I going to take accountability for what I had done? Who was going to make me accountable? I thank God for a teacher in college that told us our last semester that we had to go to counseling that semester. Boy, was I mad. Who does this chick think she is? Truth is, it saved my life. Not until you get delivered you will never know what freedom feels like. Once deliverance hit my belly, I then understood what it meant to stand in my own truth.

I preached my initial sermon on Sunday, May 5, 2013, entitled, "His character speaks for itself." The Lord allowed me to open the doors of Restored Faith Ministries on May 5, 2019. I sat with the vision in my email for 3 years before I would finally adhere to the voice of the Lord. I had preached, sang on the praise team, served various leaders, and still was ignoring this voice. It was at that moment that I ran a fever for thirty-one consecutive days and began to hallucinate. When my husband found me, he stated that I was laying prostrate praying at the front door. After being diagnosed with Lupus, I was unable to care for myself for an entire year. I began to seek God like never. I would fight my way back into the house of God not allowing anything to move me.

As much as I wanted to ignore this voice, it was getting harder and harder to do so. I had every excuse in the world and I used my father as my scapegoat. He suffered from Parkinson's, Alzheimer's, and Crohn's Disease. My reason for not doing any Ministry was because of him. One night my father fell, and I rushed him to the hospital. I would sit in anticipation for what was to come. It was not the news I wanted to hear; however, it was the place that I was supposed to be at that time. My father passed away and there were no more excuses. I printed out the name of the Ministry, By-laws, mission, and vision statements. Once I accepted the fact that I was chosen, the work began.

I served under some great leadership and then some not so great, I wondered many nights what in the world was God doing. Launching a Ministry was the last thing on my mind. Why? I had seen others go through what I was attempting to do. Who was going to help me? Who was going to show me the ropes? Who was going to attend the service? Who would install me? All the who's in the world could not prepare me for what was about to come.

No one told me that this was how things were going to be. The Holy Spirit did. Everything that I was to become or place my hand to was led only by the Holy Spirit. Yep, you better believe I got those that said, "she doesn't know what she is doing, or she is not qualified to do this and that." The truth is that hurt more than they could imagine. They said, "you had my back" and that if I needed anything "they would be there." Where the heck are they at? I had so many questions but no answers. I got to a place where I was angry with God for placing me in the wilderness with no instructions or food to enjoy while there. Little did I know there was plenty there, I just did not want it because it was not coming from the right people. You cannot hold on to folk that dropped you long before you opened your mouth. If you were supporting, giving, and doing what they needed, then you were good in their book. The minute you stopped; you were nothing to them. Truth is, you meant nothing to them in the first place. They only needed you to make them look good. The moment you started consulting God, you were defiant and did not hear from God. I had to quickly get myself together because I knew my voice was assigned to someone. The problem is they could not locate the voice because it was somewhere that did not deserve it.

As a young Pastor, I had to learn that you do not need approval from man because they did not call you. Sure, there were times that I wanted to call and ask why this or why that, but the Holy Spirit would say no. It was times that I would get in the parking lot and was not able to get out of the car. All I could do was sit in the car and cry because I really wanted to know. I cried all the way home and just wondered will this be my Ministry life. During all this, the Holy Spirit began to deal with me. I had to learn to follow the directions to the "T." I could no longer deviate from the plans that he had. I had to learn to get out of the way and let God do what he wanted to do. This meant being okay with no support from family or friends. Doing what looked crazy to them was just perfect for God. Jeremiah 29:10-11 (The Message Bible) "[10-11] This is God's Word on the subject: "As soon as Babylon's seventy years are up and not a day before, I'll show up and take care of you as I promised and bring you back home. I know what I'm doing. I have it all planned out—plans to take care of you, not abandon you, plans to give you the future you hope for." This makes so much sense once you come to the realization that God is who he says he is. Why? His plans are always perfect.

That is why I must admonish you to keep the following things in your spirit, mind, and heart.

Stay in your lane ~you cannot operate in a lane that you are not equipped to handle

Know who you are ~ never allow anyone to dictate or change who you are called to be. If you do, then you are a clone of them.

Allow the Holy Spirit to lead you ~ If the Holy Spirit did not tell you to do it, then DO NOT MOVE!

Keep your thoughts and vision to yourself ~ There are vision snatchers out there that are waiting for you to tell them what you know so that they can take it right from under you and claim that they had the idea all along. Keep some things hidden from the undertaker.

Get an understanding of the word for yourself ~ living off your grandma and mama may not be correct. Once you dive into this word and ask for revelation you just may find out what you were taught was wrong, and your understanding of a certain scripture was interpreted incorrectly.

Do not become common to the people ~ Never get so comfortable with the people that you Pastor. They should know that you are not their homegirl or homeboy. They should respect and out of the Fellowship setting. Once you common to them, they no longer respect you when you have to chastise them. Remain consistent and stand firm on your yes and no.

Learn to balance ministry versus personal life. As a leader, you must understand that you must take time for yourself. Yes, ministry must go on. However, your life does too. Commit to what you know you can handle and assign tasks to others that you can trust. Never put your expectations on others because they are YOUR expectations NOT theirs. This keeps you from being disappointed.

NEVER allow their emergency to be your emergency. Folks make time for what they choose to make time for. Even if you are a Pastor or Leader does not mean that their issue is your issue. Do not allow anyone to make you feel like you must drop everything you are doing to come to their every back and call. Do not wear yourself out trying to please everyone.

Remember, everyone's emergency is not yours. Do not make what they are going through your issue.

Author
Prophetess Donna Dandie

Donna was born in St. Andrew, Jamaica in 1965 and moved to the Cayman Islands in 1972 to be with her parents. She is the third child of nine children. She is the mother of three children and grandmother to three and is viewed as a mother by many around the world.

Although talented in several areas. She is a published author, a Special Education teacher, a workplace mediator, and a restorative practices trainer by profession with a passion for reaching out to young people, especially those who are struggling. In 2015 she was ordained as a prophet, as a Chaplain in 2016, and received an Honorary Doctorate also in 2016. She is currently pursuing a Master's in Leadership and Management. Out of her love for people and her innate desire to see people do better and go farther than she ever did, she co-founded Reach International. Through Reach International Donna reaches out to individuals from all facets of society, all over the world, including school-aged children married couples, single mothers, pastors, and spouses of pastors. She always has a word of encouragement to help individuals reach the purpose for their lives for which God intended. This multi-faceted ministry has hosted a number of conferences, training workshops, summer camps, and feeding programs, to name a few. Her ministry has led her to places like Nigeria, across the U.S.A., the United Kingdom, Amsterdam, the Bahamas, Turks and Caicos Islands, and Jamaica.

Donna stays grounded in her relationship with Yeshua, because of the individuals she ministers to. She says she sees herself in many of them in one way or another. She is not afraid to share her experiences with individuals and show her scars to Glorify Yahweh.

While she loves reading and studying just about anything she has an interest in, she says her biggest desire is to see people come to the knowledge of Yeshua Hamachiac as Lord and Savior. She truly believes that all things work together for the good of those who love Yahweh and says she is proof of that verse. She tends to be a little mischievous at times, enjoys a good laugh, and can be very animated at times.

Other than Yahweh, she attributes much of her success to her children who, she says has kept her grounded. Her relationship with each of them keeps her focused and teaches her a lot, which has made her a better person as she is often left to examine and re-examine her attitudes, behaviors, and intents because of the heart-to-heart discussion she has with her children.

Donna desires to always have a servant's heart that is fully committed to Yahweh.

MY DEDICATION

I dedicate this chapter to my children, grandchildren, and my two best friends. They are the ones who keep me grounded and challenge me when necessary. They have seen me at my most vulnerable and worst times and have never judged me. They have celebrated with me, celebrated me, and supported me, and for this, I am eternally grateful.

More so, I dedicate this chapter to Yahweh, Yeshua, and Holy Spirit. Without them, I would never dream of accomplishing what I have so far. With them, I can boast and say, "I AM A WELL-KEPT WOMAN." I love Them with my entire being.

I also dedicate this chapter to those in ministry who feel they have nowhere to turn to when they are struggling with themselves. Understand that your struggle has never dictated Yahweh's love for you, but He does desire us to be able to confront ourselves and seek help when we need it. Remember, **YOU MATTER!** May I remind you of David's words in Psalms 139:8 — *"If I ascend up into heaven, thou art there: if I make my bed in hell, behold thou art there."* Yahweh will never leave nor forsake you, so be encouraged. Blessings and love.

Connect with Prophetess Donna Dandie!

Address: P.O. Box 1151, Grand Cayman KY1-1101, Cayman Islands

Email: Reach_Intl@outlook.com

The Lady Warrior

By Prophetess Donna Dandie

"Although as children of Yahweh we are called to wholeness, until the Light of Yeshua (Jesus) fully illuminates our being, scripture alone will not suffice. To this, we must add an intimate relationship with Him, or we will continue fighting with "going back to what is familiar," for there is a war for our souls. Satan is determined to keep the darkness in, as much as Yahweh (God) is determined to expose what the darkness hides so that we can walk in total liberty."

~Donna Dandie

My name is Donna Dandie. I was born in Jamaica and moved to the Cayman Islands at around age seven. While growing up, I always felt like I did not fit in. I went through many things that I did not talk about until I was an adult because I was afraid of the repercussions of "telling."

My mother made sure that we went to church every Sunday. I was very active in Sunday School and loved helping in whatever way I could. I learned about Yahweh through watching our then Sunday School Director, Mrs. Marie Rankine. She was firm but loving and she always encouraged me to be my best. I secretly desired to be like her but convinced myself that Yahweh would never want me due to my circumstances. Nevertheless, I learned to serve because it was in serving that I found refuge. Looking back, I realize how that decision – not believing that Yahweh loved me and engaging in the act of serving as a way of escape – shaped how I responded to Yahweh for many years after I dedicated my life to Him.

It was not until I was eighteen and pregnant that I decided to follow Yeshua. I was invited to a church that met in one of the local town halls by a friend of my child's father. It was there that I decided that I had to publicly give my heart to Yahweh. Prior to that, during my Sunday School years, I felt a pull toward Yahweh, but I did not fully understand what that pull was. As a child, I can remember asking Him, "why do churches have to be separated by walls when everyone says that there is only one God?" In my child-like mind, I would envision churches without walls where anyone could walk in and hear the message, and they would be accepted. Observing the behavior of church folks made me wonder even more about Yahweh. I did not understand why people in the church were so mean to each other if they did not belong to the same denomination. This is something that bothers me to this day.

After I dedicated my life to Yahweh, based on what I heard, or interpreted, I felt that the commitment of my life was all I had to do, and everything would be perfect. I was in for a rude awakening. It was not explained to me that I had to work out my salvation and working out my salvation meant spending time to establish a personal relationship with Yeshua with the help of Holy Spirit. It was not explained to me that there would be good days and bad days, or, that I would have challenges and fall into sin, or that I would struggle with thoughts that I had to learn to take control of. I guess it was expected that I should know. It took me years to understand that I had to work out my own salvation and furthermore to understand what that even meant. When I began to understand, I realized the road that led me to work out my own salvation was messy, to say the least. Because I genuinely did not know that I had to do my part, I waited on Yahweh to change things for me. It was not until after my marriage fell apart that I began to slowly figure out I had a role to play (not to earn salvation but work out my salvation) not only for my sake but more so for the sake of my children.

My first encounter with the Holy Spirit was shortly after I committed my life to Yeshua, towards the end of my pregnancy. I was alone. I felt like an outcast, and I had no idea how I would make it. My past was still plaguing me. I did not know who I could turn to for guidance, help, or answers. So, one afternoon I walked to the seaside, which was at the end of the road I was living on, to sit on a wharf for a while. As I sat on the wharf, I started to cry. I remember my tears falling into the sea, and as I looked down into the water, I saw two small clown fishes swimming to the place where my tears had fallen. For the first time that I can recall, I heard Yahweh speak clearly to me. "The same way I take care of those fishes, I will take care of you." I dried my tears, got up, and slowly walked home. I did not know how He would do it, and it took me years to believe that Yahweh cared that much for me even though I constantly saw His hand in my life, yet deep down, I knew that I was going to be alright.

And knowing scripture was just not enough!

Earlier, I mentioned that I grew in my Christian walk believing that Yahweh would not do certain things for me. While I grew to accept that He loved me, I could not grasp the fact that He was a Father to me. My reasoning was, that maybe He is a Father to others, but not to me. I wanted Yahweh, I wanted a relationship with Yeshua, but not with a father. As a matter of fact, it took me years before I would refer to Yahweh as Father. Based on the abuse I experienced in my preteen to teenage years from individuals who were supposed to be father figures to me, I was always suspicious of anyone who would call themselves a father. So, for my own sake, I convinced myself, I had to protect myself from Him (Yahweh). I was convinced that anything special Yahweh wanted to do for me would come with a price that I would have to pay. I felt that I would have to perform for Him; that He would ask me to give something back that I was unable to give; that I would never be good enough and would always mess up; and that as a 'GREAT GOD' He would just wait for me to mess up so that He could punish me. I could not accept that His love was unconditional. I could not accept that I was worthy of His love. I could not accept that His love for me would not cause me pain and that He would never push me to do anything that was immoral or against who He is and what He stands for.

As a result, I struggled with sin for the greater part of my Christian walk. I love how The Message version of the Bible translates Romans 7:15-20:

"...I can anticipate the response that is coming: "I know that God's commands are spiritual, but I'm not. Isn't this also your experience?" Yes, I'm full of myself — after all, I've spent a long time in sin's prison. What I don't understand about myself is that I decide one way, but then I act another, doing things I absolutely despise. So, if I can't be trusted to figure out what is best for myself and do it, it becomes obvious that God's command is necessary. But I need something more! For if I know the law but can't keep it, and if the power of sin within me keeps sabotaging my best intentions, I obviously need help! I realize that I don't have what it takes. I can will it, but I can't do it. I

decide to do good, but I don't really do it; I decide not to do bad, but then I do it anyway. My decisions, such as they are, don't result in actions. Something has gone wrong deep within me and gets the better of me every time." — Rom 7:15-20 MSG

Having been raped at an early age, as well as during my young marriage, I developed some ways of thinking that would rule my life for a long time. I had a mindset that limited my personal growth. I was made to believe that if I intended to live any kind of quality life it was my responsibility to take care of the needs of others because my needs and my wants had no importance. As long as I was obedient then, I could enjoy peace. I remember being commanded by a family member to go somewhere that I knew would get me in trouble with another family member. If I did not go, I would still be in trouble. It was a matter of calculating which consequence would be the least and then going against that person. These were decisions that I had to make more often than I care to admit. When I accomplished anything that made me feel 'like somebody,' I was quickly reminded of how insignificant I was. Whatever I had received in honor of my accomplishment was either thrown away or destroyed in my presence. Having endured these situations, I took on a mindset that said, "I had no place in life, neither was I worthy of anything good from life." As a result, I learned some lessons that became my torment for many years of my life. These "life-defining moments" sounded something like this:

- → I had no say in my life.
- → Whatever was required of me was what I gave without question.
- → My body did not belong to me.
- → I had no right to say no.
- → I had no right to expect anything good for myself.
- → Anything good that came my way, I needed to find another owner for it.

And so, throughout my life, the enemy used this way of thinking in a series of events that reinforced the way I saw myself as being unredeemable, even though knowing the scriptures taught that life could and should be different. So, I set out to help others not go through what I went through, and to 'fix' those situations that I could.

I have seen through ministry, that so many times the children of Yahweh spend their time attempting to fix in others the thing that they are either unable or unwilling to fix within themselves. And we do this unconsciously many times. It is like the inability to believe in themselves as well as the dislike for what they observe in themselves drive them to 'fix others.' Almost like saying, "Well if I can't fix myself, YOU ARE GOING TO BE FIXED WHETHER YOU WANT TO BE OR

NOT." But my dear friends, this is like going into battle with ourselves. Because, if the person we are trying to fix gets better, we reinforce to ourselves that we are 'unfixable.' No wonder Matthew 7:5 warns us to "take the plank out of our own eyes before attempting to remove the speck from our brother's (or sister's eyes). In that same verse, we are addressed as hypocrites. Hypocrites because we are unable to see or face the issues in our own lives but are quick to set everyone else "straight." When we focus on fixing others and not seek to work on ourselves, we miss opportunities to truly hear from Holy Spirit and ultimately also miss opportunities to minister from a pure heart.

Here are examples of what I encountered because of my way of thinking. Even in the light of learning scripture, going to church, and hearing messages, being used by Yahweh, and seeing others delivered and set free, my own success eluded me, because I could not get away from the mental bondage I was operating under. Don't get me wrong, I saw success but not to the degree I believe I should have. I am now beginning to see through the Grace of Yahweh what I could have accomplished and what could have been, had I not held on to the debilitating beliefs that I did.

I was in relationships that went nowhere.

I found myself in a continuous cycle of relationships, whether intimate or just friendship that went absolutely nowhere. I remember in a recent conversation with a friend, he casually said to me, "you sure know how to find those people who take advantage of you, don't you?" I smiled because little did I realize at that time, this was one of the tactics that the enemy was using to keep me in bondage. I knew about the scriptures that spoke about being unequally yoked and separating ourselves from ungodly situations – but it did nothing for me. At that time, it was just words on paper.

After a while, I noticed particularly with relationships that were supposed to be headed to marriage always ended up going "south." The individuals said they were saved, but their actions over time proved differently. Most of them came with the intention of sex, and this disturbed me greatly and even though I put boundaries in place, they would push until the boundaries were no longer there.

What I realized was that when they pushed hard enough, my mind would revert right back to the helplessness I felt while raped as a child. I felt that I no longer had a right to say no, so they got what they wanted. In a strange kind of way, each time I felt that I had to prove to them that I was worth more than just sex, but my attempts never worked.

It would end up that they would go missing for a couple of weeks at a time, then come back to say "sorry" and that they wanted to make things work. I had the desire to prove I was strong and could overcome, and because I did not want to be in the dating game for long, I would believe them, and the cycle happened again and again until I had the courage to say ENOUGH IS ENOUGH.

This courage came from the knowledge that sin is sin finally getting into my spirit. I began to see how my sin hurt Yahweh and He was not pleased. I remember one day feeling like the Holy Spirit left me for good and it was the worse feeling I had ever experienced. Before I got to the state where I valued the presence of Holy Spirit more than the presence of a human being, I would always go to scriptures about adultery and fornication, felt guilty, make up my mind to change because I so badly wanted to please Yahweh and wanted Him to use me more, however, I would fall back into doing the things I despised so much. To make matters worse I could not figure out why.

The "ENOUGH IS ENOUGH" moment, is one of the greatest blessings one can enjoy. For me, it was the moment that I truly came to my senses, like the prodigal son, and reasoned that life had to be better than what I was experiencing. My Father, Yahweh, has better for me. It is coming to the place of realization that Yahweh created us to honor and be honored. But guess what? I had a whole lot of 'enough is enough' moments before getting to the big one! It is the one that shakes your core and jars you awake to the reality of what is happening and that you can really do something rather than allowing yourself to continue to play the victim.

This is the 'ENOUGH IS ENOUGH' that brings about the resolve to step out of the old clothes of sin, shame, and feeling of worthlessness, into what was accomplished through the Blood of Yeshua. This was the place where Donna had a conversation with Donna that went like this "Young lady, get your act together and stop acting like the fool you are not."

One day as I was crying out to Yahweh I heard Holy Spirit say to me, "You are seeking to find your value from someone that has no value for themselves. Furthermore, until you realize that you have been programmed as a child to give of yourself until it hurts to gain something, accept it, and give that programming to Me, then you will keep going through these cycles." While this revelation caused the change that I needed, it took a short while for it to sink in. I had never seen it that way.

I lamented and grieved, and then got angry when I realized that I had been robbed — robbed of being valued by those who should have done so - robbed of being valued by myself. You see, the question was never if Yahweh valued me. After all, he gave his son to die for my sins. Through the death of Yeshua Hamachiach, his grace and mercy kept me through all these years. It was for me to accept that truly if Yeshua lived in me according to Galatians 2:20, then I was already equipped with everything that I needed to overcome and succeed, I just had to see it and believe it for myself. This meant that I had to stop depending on others to have faith/believe for me. I had to make up my mind and do it for myself and stop being double-minded. Let me reiterate, this revelation came when I really meant, "ENOUGH IS ENOUGH."

I got it! I stood in front of the mirror one day and had a good talk with myself. I reminded myself of the work of the cross; that I had a decision to make that only I could make. I never doubted that Yahweh would use me because I made myself available to Him, what I now needed to do was to have that same level of faith that I had for others, for myself. I ended the hesitation right there at that moment - I prayed for boldness, courage, determination, and all that it took to overcome. Holy Spirit began to show me that I already had it in me. He reminded me of situations that had previously required me to step out in faith and trust Him completely, and as I did, everything turned out for His Glory in ways I would not have even thought possible. I began to accept that if I could believe that others were worthy, then so was I.

As I went through the process, I began to realize why Yahweh would tell us to love others **as** we love ourselves - because when we have no love for ourselves, we give out of nothingness, and then become discouraged that nothing is happening for us. When we do not love ourselves, we do not have the capacity to prepare our 'atmosphere' or prepare ourselves to receive love, so when good comes along, we quickly pass it on to someone else, or we abuse it and that is exactly what was happening to me.

Not only was I not loving myself, but as I encountered others, I realized they did not love themselves either, and because 'like spirits' attract 'like spirits' (meaning that the demons we struggle with - those we don't deal with attract people with similar demons into our lives), making the cycle continuous. So, the journey began. As I picked myself up along with the pieces of my broken life, I began renewing my mind about how I see myself. The scriptures took on new meaning. My relationship with Yahweh soared. I began seeing Him in everything, and I could hear Him clearly about my destiny and future.

The mindset that I had, affected me greatly in ministry. I got so caught up in not wanting anyone to go through and experience what I experienced, that the same thing that was happening to me on a personal level, began to spill over in ministry, in other words, what I experienced in the world, I started, to some extent, experiencing it in ministry as well. I was attracting the same cycles.

Now let me get this straight. Individuals will always go into ministry with their own agendas and plans which Satan can use to destroy us. But, if we are positioned properly in Yahweh and we have the Spirit of Discernment in us, we will see things for what they are, and we will deal effectively with them.

We must be aware that Yahweh is determined to complete the work He started in us. Philippians 1:6 is a wonderful reminder of this. It says, *"I am convinced and confident of this very thing, that He who has begun a good work in you will [continue to] perfect and complete it until the day of Christ Jesus [the time of His return]"* (AMP). However, sometimes we have to walk through some storms and through some fire to appreciate the importance of pursuing our wholeness so that we can be more effective in ministry.

I began to be very open in ministry about my life and the things I had been through, and even the things I was struggling with, and Yahweh used it to bless others. Yet at the same time little did I realize that Satan was orchestrating his own plan in the background and that there would arise an opportunity for someone to use the things I had shared against me in a way that almost destroyed the embodiment of who I am.

Some people will use the message they hear of your experiences to say, **"Okay, if she (or he) made it through that, I can too!" However,** others will use it to disrespect you and the anointing on your life.

I also found out that one of the greatest issues that will arise is when the spirit of familiarity sets in, and subtly those you are ministering to, begin to make themselves a little bit too familiar with you. Amid all this, because we get all caught up in our feelings, we must be willing to admit that we set ourselves up for this to happen, although unintentionally, and that was what I had to come to grips with. I had made my life available as an open book to so many people, even though I would hear Holy Spirit in the background saying, "Okay Donna, that's enough, you don't need to go that far or tell them that," but I would convince myself that because I wished others had shared a little of their journey with me through their struggles when I was just starting as a Child of Yahweh, I felt that I was doing the right thing, but I was not.

Now, I do believe that there are things about our journey that Yahweh will require us to share, but we must do so with wisdom as Holy Spirit leads. I learned the hard way that not everyone would do for me, what I would do for them.

I once encountered a situation where I had shared so much of myself, that the individual knew me inside and out because they were actively involved in the ministry Yahweh entrusted in my care. This individual was attentive to detail and was always making suggestions on how to reach more people and was faithful to their commitment. However, once as I attempted to bring about correction to a situation with the individual (to bring them back onto the path that they needed to be on) the whole thing backfired on me. I was labeled with spirits I never thought I would be accused of having. The experience almost destroyed me. It led me to a place where I was questioning my relationship with Yahweh, because I could not understand how someone so close to me in ministry would behave the way they did.

It took me months to recover and during the process of recovery, I did not stop ministering so that I could deal with the wound. I understood firsthand what leaders go through when they deal with congregants that allow Satan to use them to try and destroy the office of the leader.

We are called to minister, but who can we call to minister to us when we are blind-sided with experiences - experiences that rock us to the core and cause us to question everything we know about ourselves and our relationship with Yahweh. I realized that at times, Ministers who are going through struggles do not usually take the time they need to recover. And sometimes, there is little or no support from those closest to them to help them through difficult times. Like me, we continue to give out of a bleeding soul until we get to the place where we can give no more leading to a private meltdown with Holy Spirit. In my experience during the whole time, I was reading scriptures to build up my faith and listening to messages that reminded me of the finished work of Yeshua. I did everything I was told I should be doing or everything I thought was right, but nothing was working. On top of that, things began to go drastically wrong at work and I felt like I was going through a familiar cycle.

When I got to the point that I was ready to walk away from ministry, I told Yahweh while sobbing, that I could not do this anymore. The people I felt I needed to be there for me, were not available, and I did not want to add anything more to what they were dealing with. So, it became a lonely journey because I could not verbalize exactly what was going on in me, even with my closest friends. The day that I told Yahweh I was done with ministry, Holy Spirit said something to me ever so gently. He reminded me that there were many things that I had done in my strength to try and bring about change, and when I did it in my strength it became manipulation. That got my attention because manipulation was something that I was always so mindful of, but I could see how it became just that — I tried to manipulate circumstances so that I would not get hurt — as if I was Yahweh. I stopped and I repented. He then reminded me that I needed to look into myself and realize again, who I am in Yeshua, and that I was equipped to overcome. Then in the way that only Holy Spirit can, He had one of my best friends call to tell me not to give up and to challenge me concerning my faith in Him.

I humbled myself and had a long talk with my pastor. She listened and offered valid advice and ministered to the deepest place of my wound. I should have done this from the onset, but I found out that when something comes at you hard out of seemingly nowhere, it is so easy to forget the ones who are truly there for you.

It was that simple. I know what it is to be "bent over" and then go through the straightening process. And so again, I spoke to myself, gathered everything, and presented it all back to Yahweh. I sat and I began to see, again, the hand of Yahweh right through my entire life. And as I revisited my past testimonies, I regained the strength that I needed. So, I stood tall, and I was once again reminded that He who began a work in me, is faithful to complete it.

I cannot end this chapter without encouraging fellow Believers, especially those who are engaged in active ministry. So many times, we as ministers are innocently stoned, or we go through brokenness and guilt brought on because of our secret sins that we are unable to be honest about in the presence of someone else; we are ridiculed for our stand and beliefs; or we are just tired of giving much and being acknowledged little. For a true minister of Yahweh, it is not about the receipt of tangible things, but about receiving acknowledgment that we are doing okay, and while we know that Holy Spirit does that for us, there is just something about receiving appreciation from another genuine human being.

I want to be that voice to you today.

I know about the pain of going through the stuff that life and ministry throw at you and having to walk alone because there is no one immediately around you that you can trust to have a "boo-hoo" moment with. I know about the moments of being open, transparent, and candid about where you are at and having someone show that they are with you, but you find out that they really are not, and then they try their best to destroy you. I know about giving everything to your detriment and receiving nothing in return, or so it seems. I know about delivering messages of life to others, and inside you are dying for someone to deliver a message of life to you.

In all of this, I keep realizing something that Yahweh is so deliberate with. He shows us in His Word that it is important that we depend on Him through the study of the Word to strengthen our faith. We are equipped to be like Him, and as a result, we must find time to be refueled by Holy Spirit. This means 'relationship time' with Holy Spirit every day of our lives is what strengthens us.

I Samuel 30:6 finds David strengthening himself in Yahweh. Not someone strengthening him, he did it for himself.

Proverbs 3:5-6 tells us to trust Yahweh with our whole hearts and not to lean on our own understanding and that we should acknowledge Him in everything. I believe that many times, this has become our issue, we do not trust Yahweh totally, we do things in our own wisdom and understanding, and we do not always acknowledge Him in all we do. (I raise my own hands right here).

For I know the plans I have for you, declares the LORD, plans for welfare and not for evil, to give you a future and a hope. Then you will call upon me and come and pray to me, and I will hear you. You will seek me and

find me when you seek me with all your heart. (Jeremiah 29:11-13 ESV),

You see, many of us, and oh how I am guilty, read and quote this scripture as a show, but we do not take time to really meditate on it. Yahweh's plans for us are not just frivolous, "oh I need to do something now," plans. They are well thought out and put into place with all the necessary equipment that we need to see them operate and succeed in our lives. We need to get from quoting the scripture to the place where we are asking Yahweh,

What are your plans for me?

How do I partner with You to ensure that they come to pass?

Teach me Your ways that I may walk with you. Holy Spirit, help me to seek first Yahweh's kingdom so that all these things will be added.

For it is in seeking that we find. We find ourselves, and who we truly are in Yeshua. We find that Holy Spirit is right there waiting to guide us through and to restore us — restore our faith, hope, strength, and all we need. We find that every time we are in a place of doubt, despair, loneliness, or any other negative place, our resolve is to get up, dust ourselves, and get back on the path to continue the journey.

And so, my dear fellow co-laborers in Yeshua, keep plodding on. Yahweh needs us now more than ever before to understand who He is in us, and who we are in Him. Satan does not play fair, but Yahweh already has in place an arsenal to counteract his destructive plans and measures, and we, my dear co-laborers in Yeshua, are a part of that arsenal.

Hebrews 12:1 encourages us to lay aside every weight and the sin that so easily besets/ensnares us. Notice, that it is the weight **and** sin that causes us to lose focus. As I studied the verse, it became clear to me that:

1. We are responsible for putting aside the things that we struggle with. Scripture will guide us; and our determination will cause us to dismantle the "norms" that we have become accustomed to.
2. Realize that the weight and sin are things that the enemy places in our way to not only distract us but to trip us up to take us back to those places where we feel unworthy and separated from Yahweh.
3. We must be dependent on Holy Spirit, not only to hear Him but to also ensure that we are obedient to His instructions.

I encourage all of us that after having done all, to stand firm on the promises, and truly seek after Yahweh with our whole hearts, and not allow anything to distract us, for it is in the distraction that the enemy creeps in. I encourage us to realize that the reason the Word was not working for us (when it seemingly didn't) was not that it had no power, but because we had to intentionally reposition ourselves to see beyond the circumstances through the eyes of Yeshua with the help of Holy Spirit, and this is not always the easiest thing to do.

I end with the quote I started with —

Although as children of Yahweh we are called to wholeness, until the Light of Yeshua (Jesus) fully illuminates our being, scripture alone will not suffice. To this, we must add an intimate relationship with Him, or we will continue fighting with "going back to what is familiar," for there is a war for our souls. Satan is determined to keep the darkness in, as much as Yahweh (God), is determined to expose what the darkness hides so that we can walk in total liberty.

Be blessed. Let me say it again, **BE BLESSED.** Do not just say get in the habit of saying "I am blessed" as a cliché. **Be blessed because you are!**

Author
+Apostle Mona Lisa McCorkle

Mona Lisa McCorkle acknowledged her call to ministry in July 2002 and was licensed on October 19, 2003, under Pastor Glenn E. Mason of Emmanuel Restoration Church in Richmond, VA. On November 5, 2006, she was ordained by Apostle Karen R. Veney at Divine Will of God Ministries.

After having served at other ministries in various capacities, in March 2012, God called her into pastoral office and charged her with founding New Hope Restoration Ministries — a ministry of hope and restoration. She was consecrated and commissioned in the Office of Apostle on June 6, 2015. A little less than a year later, God sent her to North Carolina where she has founded and leads The Garden Worship and Outreach Center in Eden, N.C.

Apostle Mona Lisa is married to Eugene B. McCorkle III. She gave birth to a woman warrior, Lauren Manns, and has one grandchild. She holds a bachelor's degree in Administration of Justice, a master's degree in Human Service

Counseling, and completed her second master's degree in Ministry in 2020.

Apostle Mona Lisa is an entrepreneur; she is the owner of School of Thought, LLC, providing training, workshops, and coaching for individuals, small businesses, or corporate organizations. She hosts retreats, conferences, and workshops. In addition, she is a licensed NC Realtor/Broker with Allen Tate Realtors. Apostle McCorkle is also a Board member of the CORMII Community Development Corporation, Reidsville, NC, and has served on the leadership team of the Rockingham County Racial Equity Learning Community. She released her first CD single in 2020 entitled, "Breathe."

Apostle Mona Lisa loves the Lord with all her heart and desires to walk upright, operate with integrity, and please Him. A scripture she stands on is Romans 8:28,

"And we know that all things work together for good to those who love God, to those who are the called according to His purpose."

My Dedication

I thank God for giving me the desires of my heart and for being the good, good Father that He is. I have been a writer since I was twelve years old, but I have never authored a published book, until now. I first dedicate this work to God for He has been my sustainer through every hill and valley.

I dedicate this chapter to the memory of my mother, Elder Marjorie Louvenia Broadnax Price. She never allowed us to say, "I can't." After assuring us that we could, she would quote Philippians 4:13 to us; it has remained with me throughout my life. Thank you for demonstrating to us what true faith and wisdom look like. Thank you for exemplifying a well-lived life of a follower of Jesus Christ. Thank you for being both my physical and my spiritual mother. I will see you later.

I further dedicate this chapter to my dear husband, Eugene B. McCorkle, III. You are my supporter, encourager, pusher, cheerleader; and you also make me believe I can do anything. I so appreciate your gentle and quiet, yet strong nudges, and for holding me accountable for all I say I am going to do or desire to do. I thank you, and I love you beyond words.

To my Lauren and Myles, my Carmen, Amanda, and Janet; and my Takiyah, I dedicate this, my first published written work, to you. You love me, support me, push me, allow me to be me, and pray for me. I am grateful that you trust the God in me. I love each of you more than words can express.

Finally, to every reader who has accepted God's call to ministry, I dedicate this chapter to you.

"And let us not grow weary while doing good, for in due season we shall reap if we do not lose heart."

Galatians 6:9 (NKJV)

Connect with Author Apostle Mona Lisa by visiting:

Website: https://theschoolofthoughtllc-nc.com

Email: monalisamccorkle@allentate.com

Email: apostlemlisamccorkle@gmail.com

Instagram: mlisamccorkle

Facebook: The Garden Worship and Outreach Center, Inc.

(thegardenatedennc)

YouTube: Light it Up with Mona Lisa

4

The Process of the Journey:

I Was Graced for This

By Apostle Mona Lisa McCorkle

9 Then the Lord stretched out His hand and touched my mouth, and the Lord said to me,
"Behold (hear Me), I have put My words in your mouth.
Jeremiah 1:9

The answer "yes" to the call of ministry is nothing to be taken for granted or to be taken lightly. When God's calling and purpose for your life include shepherding His people and establishing ministries, you better know *Him*! You must know that *He* called you, and set your eyes, heart, and mind on *Him*, as *He* is and will be your most important, significant, and impactful model for ministry and leadership.

But do not allow the simplicity of that opening paragraph fool you. It (the calling) is a lot; it's a whole lot. I have heard so many people (who either have not been called or have not acknowledged or chosen to walk in their calling) talk about ministers and ministry. Frankly, unless you have done the work, you will never understand the bittersweetness that comes with holding, lifting, and drinking this cup. If I had really known what I would be in for when accepting this call, would I have really said, "Yes?" I would like to think so, but in all honesty, I cannot be certain.

I sometimes think about October 19, 2003, when I was licensed into the ministry of the Gospel of Jesus Christ. My mother, Marjorie Louvenia Broadnax Price, the greatest human model of Christianity and Christ that I have ever known, introduced me before I brought forth the Word that day. In that introduction, she said something that has stuck with me since:

She shared that she always knew that God had great work for me to perform.

She further stated that it was evident, even from the early stages of my life, that the enemy did not want me to live. While I was in her womb, she almost lost me (I was the first child she had given birth to after having experienced several previous miscarriages.) Then she shared that even after my birth, during my infancy that I almost died (again) because of some paint fumes that were in the house. Those were just a couple of examples that she shared, but oh, there have been so many other examples and so many other challenges that I have faced — just because I said,

"Yes." My "yes" is still "yes!"

You see, I did not just arrive here. I neither thought about nor imagined being called to the ministry of the Gospel. Furthermore, when people would say that I had a pastoral calling on my life, I would hold up both of my forefingers, crossing them while making an "X," and saying that I did not want any parts of such and that was *not* my calling. Little did I know that God had already planned it.

I never ran from the acknowledgment and acceptance of the call of ministry; I just wanted to be certain that I heard God clearly for myself, not based on what anyone else had spoken. Believe me, many great prophets had spoken over me. My Mama had a saying, though: "Some were called; some were sent, and some just went." I love God with my whole heart, and, even then, I desired to be obedient to His instruction, but I was *not* going to be one of those who *just went*.

I had been a part of the church in which I was licensed since 1998 when it was founded. I served on the praise team and experienced life transformation at that church. Our Pastor was one who spent time with God; he knew and preached the word. When he preached, the power of the Holy Spirit was present; I became convicted about some of the things that I was doing - one of the most pivotal moments happened when I stopped clubbing.

Looking back at that time, I shake my head because of the audacity I sometimes had. I was a bold somebody! Bold and bad! I recall having a conversation with some of the older ladies of the church one time when we were all at an event for the youth. As I look back on it now, how could I dare be so arrogant? Who did I think I was? I told them that I had been delivered from everything else, but I was not even trying to be delivered from sex (outside of marriage since I was single during that time). It seemed as though the minute that I spoke that out of my mouth, God started dealing with me. Y'all, I threw away *my* Black Book – YES, I had one! During my time at that ministry, I obtained my freedom; I was set free! I remember being so excited when I received the baptism of the Holy Spirit, which empowered my walk and my calling even greater.

One night, I came home after having participated in Bible Study. I sat on the side of my bed and wept almost uncontrollably because my spirit was longing for more. There was something more that I was needing. My *yes* had caused me to be hungry! I wanted to know more. I wanted God more. After having experienced such growth and transformation, it became evident that I had received all that God had for me to receive from that place. I loved them dearly, but I knew in my Spirit that there was more. I will forever appreciate the fire and growth that I experienced there. There is order in departure, however. Therefore, I met with my pastor to share what Holy Spirit had spoken to me regarding my leading and received a proper release.

God had previously connected me to someone who would become a dear friend. I had no idea that she would play such a significant role in my ministry walk and purpose. She became my first mentor when I accepted the call, but even more than that, she was my first teacher (other than my mother) who demonstrated what God's power looked like through a yielded vessel. Yes, I did say *she*; she was a woman. God used her mightily! He continues to use her mightily. My mama taught me not to move by man's instruction but by God's instruction; I waited and listened. God instructed me to go be a part of the teaching, training, and ministry of this woman who had mentored me. I knew it was of God; He had answered my prayer for more. Little did I know how impactful this move would be for ministry and for God's calling on my life. Later, in 2006, she would ordain me as an Elder and trust me with a position of oversight within the ministry. I witnessed her example of how God used yielded vessels to operate in deliverance; this was where I became interested in and learned about deliverance ministry.

God had sent her back to Virginia to build. When she was consecrated and affirmed in the Office of the Apostle, she became the first Apostle I had known personally. Frankly, I did not even know what an Apostle was at the time. I was reared in the Baptist church, and Lord knows, I appreciate my strong, solid foundation, but the only Apostles that were talked about were the twelve Apostles – no more, no less. So, *what* in the world was an Apostle in this modern church?

Though I did not fully understand at the time, I would later come to realize that this Apostle demonstrated the characteristics of the Apostle; she established; she trained; she equipped; she set order, and God's power was evident as she taught and ministered. My being a part of this ministry and serving under her tutelage was necessary for my process and understanding my calling. I served in that ministry for about three years. There I was content and happy to serve as an Elder; I had found my place. I simply wanted to help others build their ministries. Subsequently, I served as Elder at two other churches and had a passion and desire for training leadership. At one place, it was received; at another, it was not. My experience at the latter is something that I never imagined that I would experience in ministry. We hear so much about church hurt, and with all that I have experienced in ministry, especially in *that* church, I have never called it *church* hurt. It was the people in the church who hurt me; it was not the church. Unfortunately, the greatest hurt came from the Pastor. I would never attempt to expose him by providing details; God knows the details. I have forgiven although no such request was ever made. All is well.

For those who have never been called (or answered the call), it is so easy to criticize those who are doing the work. When I served as Elder in one of the ministries, there were so many things that I did not understand. I respected the Pastor, but I did not understand his leadership style. I recall writing a letter when it was time for me to leave that ministry. In that letter, I wrote some things that I believed, at the time, were constructive statements for the Pastor. I really thought I knew what I was talking about. I did it with the best intentions. There is something my mama used to say, though, "The road to Hell is paved with good intentions." Years later, after I had experienced the pastoral calling, the Holy Spirit instructed me to send a letter of apology to the pastor for some of the misguided statements I had made. At the time I thought I had been right, but the Holy Spirit showed me that I was wrong. I wrote the letter and mailed it to him.

Never be too big or too prideful to apologize... to anyone.

Being in right standing with God has been and is my desire. I never want to be found prideful. I will always apologize if I have said or done something to someone that was wrong, spoken in the wrong tone, or spoken from a place of misunderstanding. I will be the first to apologize. I want nothing to separate me from my peace with God.

I recall, so vividly, one Sunday in 2012. It was around the last Sunday in January. That morning the Lord told me to drive to Tappahannock, VA (I then lived in Chesterfield, VA) to visit the church of an Apostle and Prophetess that I had met. Obediently, I made the hour drive — was even pulled over by a State Trooper while on the way there — but was extended grace that I requested of him. Something that I will never forget happened that day. Only the Apostle, Prophetess, their grandson, and my husband and I were present for service that day. God had designed it all. As we worshiped, the fire of God filled us and the sanctuary. They began to prophesy. The last thing I remember taking place, though, was this: the Prophetess placed her hands on my belly and said, "The Lord said *now* is the time for you to give birth."

I trusted the Prophetess and the word from God, and I was thinking, "Oh, okay, God." I thought I was going to wait a few more months until He gave me instructions for the next thing to do. I was so wrong! The next day, He instructed me to go by a little shopping center area that was behind my neighborhood. I remember driving and saying out loud,

"Lord, I'm going in obedience, but I ain't trying to start no church." I rode around the building and saw that there were no vacant building units. I then proceeded to pull out of the parking lot when I heard somebody call my name — loudly: "ELDERRRR!" "Who in the world is in here that knows me," I thought. This, indeed, was a God moment! It was a ministry colleague that I had known from the ministry in which I was ordained. I had no idea at the time, but she operated her beauty salon in that building. She had seen and recognized my car and rushed to catch me before I had driven out of the parking lot.

Little did I know the set-up that God had awaiting me. I remember her saying, "God sent you here for me; I've got you. You can use my building." Mind you, we were in a hair salon. I was looking perplexed, "What we gon' do; move the bowls back?" She laughed and said, "No, I've got another building." Well, God had me in for a shock with that one! We met at her "other" building on that Wednesday. When she opened the door, and I saw the space, I knew it was God. The space was already set up for church. She blessed us with that space, for which we were not asked to pay rent - only what we were blessed to give.

I had heard so many stories from people in ministry who talked about being broke, spending their own money to pay for ministry (to the point to which they were unable to pay for their own needs). Though I had heard the stories, I do not know anyone else's story like I know my own. However, I do know this:

I told God that my Yes would always be Yes.

Then I asked Him something - I asked Him that as long as I am obedient to what He instructs me to do, would He not allow my household finances to be in lack as a result of my taking on this call of Pastor in ministry and founding a new church. I guess that was very bold of me, but I tell you, He has never let it happen. My household has not suffered financially because of ministry.

Leaders, be wise with church money! Be good stewards over God's money; it is His money, not ours. I do not believe that God intends for us to be bound and broke while we are leading folk! If we seek God, hear God, and move according to God's instruction (and not our own desires), He will always provide. I believe in operating in a spirit of excellence in all that I do — especially those things that God has assigned to my hands. We have to learn how to follow the specific instructions for what God tells us to do, with no deviations. He will cause favor and blessings to fall from places you could never imagine.

From the nice, cushioned chairs that our ministry in Virginia purchased, God did it! A member told me that God told her to make a deposit into our account for the cost of all the chairs, and that was what she did. When you are a leader of integrity and you preach God's Word, He will cause people to pour into your ministry. We were given land by a total stranger. If I saw him today, I would not know who he is. The church still owns it. That is the God that I believe in for ministry. He has never given me vision without provision. Early in ministry, when I committed my life and the ministry to Him, I learned to trust Him for the process, as well as provision. He has never failed us!

When I begin to think about ministry, I share so many of the wonderful experiences I have had over the past nearly eighteen years. Even before I was licensed, my Pastor released me to begin ministering at the prisons for women in Virginia. That was my purpose and my passion for about thirteen years. I will never forget the salvation and deliverance that were experienced in those prisons during service. I am still amazed that God chose and still chooses to use me. Most people do not know my name, but God does, and He is the one Who matters!

Unfortunately, the picture of my calling, my anointing, my apostle-ing is not all good. There are things that I contend with. I have been talked about. I have been misunderstood. I have been perceived wrongly and lied to, however, it has not deterred me. Many people say they *know* me, but they lie. If you have never had a full conversation with me or have never broken bread with me, or we have never engaged in anything at all, you simply know of me or about me. I often think of how Jesus must feel. So many people say they *know* Him when they are only casual acquaintances...and then He has to squint from a distance just to see who they are. Ha!

I digress. I think one of the biggest revelations I have received in ministry leadership has been this:

No matter the oil, no matter the cost, no matter the sacrifice, no matter if they have acknowledged you in private, some people (family, friends, strangers all included) will never recognize you for who you are in the Kingdom because God made you a woman!

I would be lying if I said that it did not hurt or bother me (especially when I have experienced it from a family whom I love and who, themselves, are ministers and pastors of the Gospel). It is temporary discomfort. I know God called me. Not only did He call me, but He also designed me as Apostle and leader even before I was known on Earth. That is what I love about this walk - it is His purpose and plan, and He chose me to walk it out.

Prior to my being consecrated and affirmed as Apostle, I was hungry to know exactly *what* this thing was and *how* I could be sure that it was truly me. I was hungry because I could not answer a call of which I knew nothing. I am so glad God knew. Out of what seemed like nowhere, Holy Spirit led me to a website I had never heard of, and I read about Apostle Collette Toach and the Five-Fold Ministry School. The introduction to that school and to the apostleship wrecked my everything!

The first course that I took was entitled "Apostolic Foundations." The course provided sound Biblical instruction regarding the calling and the purpose of the Apostle, as well as facilitating my taking an introspective examination of my life. The course should have taken about two to three months to complete. It took longer, though. At one point early in the course, the content and the assignments became extremely personal and deep — so much so that I could not move forward; I had to stop. It delved deeply into me, my childhood, my relationships, my private things. I put it away for a few months. When I came back to it, ready to release and to receive, the inner work that took place, along with the work of the Holy Spirit inside of me, resulted in transformation and great understanding. I, then, truly knew who I was, why I acted the way I did, why I had to be raised the way I was raised, and what I had been called to do.

So, yes, I am sure. I am an Apostle. God called me that. I have heard people often say, "The title doesn't matter." What they do not understand is this:

The oil that comes with such calling matters.

Unless one is called to be an Apostle, he or she cannot fully understand the cost of such a calling and anointing. I think back to the letter that I wrote to my former Pastor (that I previously referenced). It was not until I walked in the shoes of a Pastor and served as a Pastor that I understood the oil and the grace that came with the pastoral office.

I love praying with people almost as much as I love eating, and that is a lot. They call; I pray – because I love prayer. I now realize that I have been oblivious or naive to some things, though. During 2020 and 2021, I received more calls for prayer than ever. When people were placed in the hospital because of COVID or when they were just *going through* or just needed spiritual insight and strength, I listened, I prayed, I did.

What amazes me, though, is this: some of the same people that I have prayed for, pushed through, held counseling sessions with, do not support me or approve of me as a woman leader/Apostle and are a part of other churches and ministries, yet, they say that the Holy Spirit told them to call me. I know I am older but sometimes still a bit naive. God forbid if they ever received revelation from God Himself that He did not just appoint men as ministry leaders but women too. God forbid I say *Apostle*; I now realize that most of them know very little, if anything, about the Office, the Calling, and the Work and ministry of the Apostle. I did not sign up for this cup, but I drink it daily.

I bet I am learning, though! There won't be a long line of phone calls for prayer in 2022. I am going to ask them this question:

Who is *your* leader, Pastor, Apostle?

I have been through so much more than these pages can hold, but I will not complain. Every trial has taught me a lesson or made me stronger (ultimately). They did not feel good to my flesh, but they worked together for good for my journey. God has graced me for this work, and I will continue to live beyond Monday.

Author
+Apostle Reveena M. Blair

Apostle Reveena Blair is a native of Portsmouth, Virginia. Since her youth, she has been known as a vessel for God and a lover of community and people.

Blair accepted the call on her life to preach the gospel of Jesus Christ in June 2004. This call quickly transitioned from being licensed to becoming the Minister of Music for the church she attended during that time. As time progressed, she was later licensed as an Evangelist and later affirmed as Apostle.

For anyone that knows Apostle Blair, they would tell you that she is a relentless worshiper! She has a heart to serve and is a fierce advocate for community, evangelism, and recovery. She serves as the Founding Pastor and Visionary of New Beginning Evangelistic Ministries in Winston-Salem, North Carolina. Since founding this ministry she also covers two thriving ministries in Augusta, Georgia and Tupelo, Mississippi through The House of Restoration, a vision also birthed through her.

Finally, Apostle Blair is a global voice, atmosphere shifter and the proud mother of three children, one grandchild and several spiritual children and mentees.

"Make it a GREAT DAY, because you can

COMMAND YOUR DAY!"

-Apostle Reveena M. Blair

My Dedication

I dedicate this literary work to my daughter, Maya. I have endured the process, so that you will never have to.

I love you, Beautiful!

To connect with Apostle Reveena Blair:

Facebook: New Beginning Evangelistic Ministries

Email: newbeginningem1@gmail.com

Phone: (336) 602-9008

5

The Process

By Apostle Reveena Blair

I have been asked this question many times – "If you knew then what you know now about ministry, would you still answer the call?"

Good question.

My name is Apostle Reveena Blair, and I am the founder and senior pastor of New Beginning Evangelistic Ministries located in Winston Salem, North Carolina. I am also the founder of The House of Restoration, which oversees three other ministries in other states. I have been in ministry for roughly seventeen years, and a Pastor for eleven of those years. As rewarding as this calling has been, experience has shown me that it does not get any easier with time.

I was not necessarily raised in church, but I do, however, come from a family with great faith and believers. My birth mother, who is the prophet of our church, has been able to see and hear the voice of God for as long as I can remember. She is a woman of great wisdom and understanding. She taught us what great faith is by using her own experiences and what we saw her go through and overcome as well.

In the past I would go to church with a family member. Every time I went to church, the Pastor would ask me to sing. At that time, I was not living a lifestyle that was pleasing to God. I did not even try to have a real relationship with God at all, I just knew He was there. My level of relationship with Him was evident, as I only called on Him when I needed Him. **Despite my motive,** He allowed it because that was how we connected. I would sing with my eyes closed, shutting out everything and every distraction. I would be so much in my own world that I did not realize the moments that I helped in someone else's deliverance. I used to say to myself, "this song is for me!" Whatever I sang about, I made it personal.

I remember the exact day the Holy Ghost came upon me. I was around nineteen years old and thought I was running the world. I was taking a shower and singing as I usually did when God grabbed ahold of me. It was as if the words to the song came alive within me. I felt warm all over and could not control what was happening within me. I could not stop crying as I repented with a pure heart and my tears became one with the water flowing down the drain. The gift of tongues was given to me right on the floor of my shower. What an experience that was for me! I will never forget that moment. This place in my life showed me just how real God was and how much He truly loved me.

When I TRULY said yes to God, it was the best choice I had ever made for myself. I caught fire for God and all I wanted to do was serve. I literally started at the bottom but did not mind that one bit. I loved my leader and understood what she had in her belly and on her tongue was needed for my growth. I knew that she was a watchman over my soul, so whatever I could do to make her life easier that was what I did. I wanted her to brag about me to God. I served with gladness and did my best to do so with a spirit of excellence.

The first time I heard the voice of God, He simply said the word, "usher." I was excited to hear Him speak to me, but I had no idea what to do next. I ran to my leader, and with the biggest smile on her face she looked at me and said,

"Yes, you heard Him correctly."

So, I did my assignment with a smile. I ushered at the door, and I cleaned the church; whatever was needed, I did it without hesitation. I also joined the praise and worship team, and eventually became the praise team leader, too. As my relationship with God grew, I became more passionate about the ways of God. When my leader told me that God said it was elevation time, it blew me away. Within what felt like minutes, I became the minister of music. Honored that the

Father had given me such a task, I learned all I could about the position. Just as I served my leader, I served and submitted to God even more. I knew that what He had entrusted me with was heavy but had to be carried by me. When you truly love God, you do not want to disappoint him.

By my third or fourth year in ministry, I was allowed to put together services by inviting other preachers to come and minister at our church. I also led various outreach programs that provided food for children and families in low-income housing and to people who were experiencing homelessness. I always brought someone new to church. I had a street ministry like no other and I love to help people. After a while, I was again elevated, but this time to Evangelist.

God eventually shifted my family and I to North Carolina. This time, I answered the call to Pastor. I want to be clear - this is not something that I wanted to do. I saw a lot of what my leader went through, and I wanted no parts in that. After I was installed, I continued to sit in the back of another Pastor's church. I was afraid to go forward. God will certainly make you uncomfortable in a place where you do not belong. I was eventually pushed to start New Beginning right in my living room. Three years later, but still before I was ready, I was affirmed as an Apostle of the Lord's Church.

There is a great process one must go through to be granted access to different realms of the spirit, and I am not talking about titles. When a minister goes forth before their time, they are denied access to various things spiritually or may begin to use their gifts illegally. I have seen so many "fake it till you make it" pastors. They end up burned out or beat down by taking on assignments or demons they were not prepared for. I have learned that the timing of God is everything. This taught me some very important lessons. Still nothing could prepare me for the loss, hurt and persecution I have dealt with along the way. This is a teacher's journey. You will never stop learning because God is always downloading.

I have lost so much along the way that it saddens me at times. I still push forward and do what God has instructed me to do. There was always that push in my back every time I wanted to give up or quit and always an encouraging word, from my leader given that strengthened me to go a little bit further. So of course, I stayed in the race while broken; all I knew was ministry! I dealt with great loss, sickness, divorce and much more but there was never a free moment for me to heal ME; the call held my complete attention no matter what storm I had to fight through.

As I kept going, God mended and healed me right under the church's nose. God was certainly with me every step of the way. I want to share with you some experiences I went through and some hits I have taken because of my YES. I am hoping something in these pages will help you along your journey. It still amazes me when I see so many leaders running to start a church or to receive a title. I literally say to myself "if they only knew what comes next, many would not pursue it."

When I first started pastoring, I made more than a few mistakes, which was to be expected. The Holy Ghost is a great teacher but the experience you go through will make sure you never do certain things again. Now my words are not here to deter you from answering the call that is on your life, but simply to help you understand that it is not something you take lightly! You must understand the cost of the oil and the benefits of being a part of the kingdom citizenship.

Everyone has a "why" story. Why did I come to God? Why did I choose to be in ministry? If you do not, then you should really sit in consideration of what all He has done for you. What is your why story? Ministry is not for the faint of heart. This is not the move to make just because you are a great speaker or pastoring runs in your family. You cannot do this for the accolades or to have an "Amen" corner. Before I begin my list of wisdom for you, this truth deserves to be repeated:

You must be called to ministry.

The warfare alone will hurt you in more ways than one if you go for any other reason. Your faith must already be at a level that you trust God with everything. There are many leaders who are dead and never became the very thing that God spoke over their lives. Knowing what you can handle in your life is just as important as the faith you have. The weight of ministry is heavy, so your WHY must be God-led and not "self-led." When I was reconciled back to God, I fell in love. In love with a God that singled me out and pulled me from a pit. A dark pit I created for myself.

So, what fueled my pursuit of God? The truth is – knowing all that I had survived!

I lived a very wild lifestyle that only God could redeem me from. I was gang raped at the age of thirteen years old and my life spun out of control. I did not care about much of anything after that. I became a female pimp who exploited women for money. If it was not about money, it did not make sense to me. I was also addicted to cocaine at the early age of fourteen. Even when I was surrounded by people, I was still constantly alone and severely depressed. I begin to look for anything and anyone to call my own and fill the void.

There is no greater love than what God shown me. Saying yes to God was the least I could do, after all, He saved my life, while I was trying to destroy it.

[a]Therefore I urge you, [b]brothers and sisters, by the mercies of God, to present your bodies [dedicating all of yourselves, set apart] as a living sacrifice, holy and well-pleasing to God, *which is* your rational (logical, intelligent) act of worship. — Romans 12:1

My why may not be your why but I promise the Father has saved us all. He gave us the ultimate sacrifice, His Son, Jesus! How can I not serve a God like that? The things I have gone through while in ministry have certainly taken a toll on me physically, emotionally, and spiritually but my answer is still YES.

I have four rules I live by now concerning my life.

1. My first rule is simply, to always take care of you first. You are no good to anyone when you are broken down. I believe in leading while bleeding but certainly not while dying. There is a huge difference between the two as God showed me. I have claimed victory over cancer three times. Going through divorce, I almost lost my mind. I have constantly had to put band-aids on cuts from people who say they love me and left me distrustful. We are certainly tried by the fire, but you must be strong enough not to fold. God never said the weapon would not form; but He did say it will not prosper. Every hit you take shows yourself and God strong.

2. My number two rule is to treat others how you want to be treated, not how they treat you. This is the hardest rule for me. Oh, the stories I could tell of Pastors scandalizing my name, the once sons and daughters turning on me and lying on me or the Facebook rants simply because someone would not get their way, or their feelings got hurt. I have cried myself to sleep many nights. I could not respond or defend myself because God simply said, "silence." When I tell you, I almost lost my salvation many times and even thought jail would be worth me tearing up somebody. I thank God for the Holy Spirit dwelling on the inside of me. He will keep you from acting like them. So, remember hold your peace. Find a way to kill them with kindness, without being a pushover. Let God fight your battles because you will not win without him.

3. **The third rule of mine is you cannot do this alone.** It is an old saying I will not go if I have to go by myself. God never sent anyone out alone. Make sure your team is trustworthy and stable. Stability in God gives you ABILITY with Him. It is hard to trust people who are easily moved by people or situations. Train them before you put them to work. Make sure they understand the weight of the mantle and ministry.

Also having the correct covering is necessary. Spiritual parenting is certainly shown in the Bible in multiple places. As leaders we must be poured into as we pour into others. We are all still learning, we must be taught, guided, prayed for, and pushed just as much.

Every great leader must know how to be humble and follow before one can ever lead. There were many times I was mad at my leader, but I never stepped out of place. Can you still show up when you are upset? Do not move off your emotions. They will have you in a ditch. God certainly does not move because we are in our feelings but instead, He moves out of our faith, obedience, and willingness towards Him.

4. Last but certainly not least, rule four is, do not rush the process. Do not move too fast. What is for you, is for you. If God said it, then that settles it. You do not have to run towards anything - just keep showing up and be obedient to the voice of God. Philippians 4: 6-7 Be anxious for nothing. We must make preparation for every door that God wants us to walk through. We must be groomed and taught before we can groom and teach others. As you elevate it is like putting on a pair of pants you cannot quite fit. They are not hanging off, yet they do not fit the way you want them too either. To fill your pants will take your own experiences and God's guidance through this place of humility and learning.

To answer the question, "If I knew then what I know now would I still answer the call?" I absolutely would. I made up my mind that pleasing God is all that matters; to have the heart for God's people and to see people how He sees them not how we see each other. I can tell a young mother with certainty that I know she can make it and that there is help and tell a young man that he does not have to sell drugs to take care of his family. I was that young mother, that drug dealer, and the cocaine user, too. I now stand as a testimony, one who can tell them that help available. The small battles do not matter much when you know there is a victory in the end. The Word of God says this:

"For I reckoned that the sufferings of this present time are not worthy to be compared with the glory which shall be revealed in us."

Romans 8:18

Yes, we may go through, but it will all be worth it at the end. I pray in reading this it has made you think and encouraged you along the way. Stay the course and go all way with God.

Author
Minister Shakirah Green

With a heart full of sincerity and love for the Kingdom of God, and now a three-time published author, this fascinating woman of God has been blessed beyond measure. In the area of gifts and talents that she enjoys sharing with the world in her own unique "out-of-the-box" type of way.

Not only is she an anointed vessel for Christ, but she also humbly serves others with a great deal of compassion because she understands that she would be absolutely nothing without her Lord and Savior. Whether she is making others laugh with her sense of humor or teaching vocals with a twist, she aims to make a difference in the lives of those around her by exemplifying the love of God. This mother, wife, minister, sister, aunt, author, business owner, recording artist, musician, vocal coach, poet, public speaker, and borderline comedian is better known as Shakirah Nicole Green, and she is beyond grateful to have this opportunity to share with you.

Author Shakirah Green's Literary Works:

CALL A SPADE A SPADE
https://bit.ly/AUTHORSHAKIRAHSPADEBOOK

BROTHER MAN, SISTER GIRL
https://bit.ly/AUTHORSHAKIRAH2

To connect with Minister Shakirah Green:

Shakirah Nicole Green

704.665.7484

Tehillah Academy

the.tehillah.academy@gmail.com

DX Professional Services

dxprofessionalservices@gmail.com

My Dedication

Wearing several hats, which consists of great responsibilities that may seem insurmountable, is not an easy task; with it comes stress, frustrations, an overwhelming feeling of doubt and fear of failure, and the like. It takes an extraordinary individual to deal with the pressure of it all, hence my dedication to the most amazing woman in my life. My mother, Apostle Bobbie Jackson, has been my SHE-RO. She has and will always be the mentor, the confidant, the instructor, the chastiser, the encourager, the builder, the motivator, the cheerleader, the role model, and the best mother that any daughter could ever dream or pray of having in her life.

She has believed in me when I did not have the confidence to believe in myself.

She has pushed me to accept the ministry within me when I did not believe I was worthy enough to carry any form of mantle.

She has taught me to continue pressing despite of the hinderances and hurdles that life may present and, because of her tenacity to see me be great, I am able to push past obstacles to witness my hopes and dreams manifest.

Even the more, my children will be able to witness the outcome of what my mother has instilled in me so that they may do the same.

Mommy, from the deepest sentiments of my heart, THANK YOU! Your Teddy will ALWAYS cherish you, both now and forever!

6

WHEN THE MIC DROPS: TRUTH BEHIND THE SCENES
By Minister Shakirah Green

"Woman of God, lift your hands. God is calling you to a higher place in Him. He's going to use you in mighty ways. You are more than just a singer and a minister, you're a Prophet of God. You're going to preach the Gospel to the world. Your gift will make room for you. Your name will be a household name to millions. You are a prophet to the nations."

There I stood. Frozen. Shocked. Speechless. *Who me?* They must be mistaken. There is no way in the world that I am going to preach to the world or prophesy to the nations. I will sing all day long, that comes easy, but PROPHESY?! Yeah right. I immediately remembered what my mother had told me a while back about prophetic words being spoken over my life. So, I said to myself, "Nope, ain't accepting that one, i'm good," but there was one thing that I *did* forget:

Running from purpose will only prolong the fulfillment of my destiny but it will never erase it; nevertheless, I kept running and man did I run.

I ran like Forest Gump! Little did I know that the very same day that prophetic word was spoken over my life, my life would never be the same. Despite my running, despite my rejection of the call on my life, despite my disobedience to surrender my will, I could not shake what I heard.

Days passed.

Weeks passed.

Months passed.

I still could not shake it. I would try to sleep at night but would be awakened at sometimes two and three o'clock in the morning. No, I did not have to use the restroom. No, the alarm clock was not set to wake me up that time of morning. So, why in the world was I up so early? Then, it dawned on me as I pressed rewind in my mind that this was the exact same thing that happened to me as a little girl.

I remember distinctly at the darkness of dawning one morning, at the age of twelve, as I laid in my bed, and heard my name being called. I jumped up out of bed, walked to my parent's bedroom door and knocked. They permitted me to enter, and I asked, "Mommy, did y'all call me?" She said, "No, we didn't call you." So, I went back to bed. A few moments later, I heard my name being called again, so I repeated my steps. I walked to my parent's bedroom door and knocked. I was permitted to enter, and I asked again.

"Mommy, did y'all call me?" She said, "No, we didn't call you." So, once again, I went back to bed and closed my eyes. But then, a few minutes later, "Shakirah." I got up and walked to my parent's door. I knocked, and after being permitted to enter, I asked my mother again. "Mommy, did y'all call me?" At that very moment, my mother realized that it was the voice of God calling my name. My mother gave me the same instructions that Eli had given to Samuel. She said,

"The next time you hear your name being called say out of your mouth, 'Speak Lord, for thy servant hears.'"

I was puzzled, but I was obedient. I walked back to my bedroom, climbed into the bed, and got underneath the covers. I snuggled myself and got comfortable. I closed my eyes and drifted off to sleep until a sweet soft voice spoke, "Shakirah." I remember taking a deep breath and obeyed the instructions given. "Speak Lord, for thy servant hears." Immediately, there was a cool but soothing breeze that brushed my face. Suddenly, an overwhelming need to cry filled my spirit followed by tears that I could not control. I had no idea what was taking place. I ran to my parent's room and knocked. It was as if my mother already anticipated that something had taken place. I walked into my parent's room and with tears in my eyes, I said "Mommy, I heard my name again, and I did what you told me to do. Mommy, I can't stop crying." My mother looked at me with joy in her eyes and told me that I, for the first time, was experiencing a personal encounter with God. She grabbed my hands and began to pray with me. It was at that moment that my mother knew that I was not only called but chosen of God. I was still somewhat clueless as to what was happening within me, but one thing that I absolutely knew without a doubt was that what I was feeling at that moment was a feeling that I would not mind experiencing again.

Not too soon after that encounter, at the age of thirteen, I was asked to be the guest speaker at a youth service. *Who me?* I suddenly adopted a Moses spirit. I did not know how to speak to people! Singing in front of a crowd was different. It was easy for me to sing to large groups. But to speak, like speak in front of people and not just in the shower to myself? Just the thought of being in a church filled with people, not just adults but kids my age, made me scared out of my mind, but I remembered the "Yes" I had given the Lord, and I could not take it back, besides, my mother told me that I couldn't (LOL). When the day of the youth event approached, I was so nervous that my nerves were nervous.

How am I going to be able to do this?

The drive to the guest church seemed like it only took two minutes. What in the world? That was the shortest thirty-minute drive in history. As I entered the church, many began to smile and shake my hand. With all the warmth of the welcome and encouraging words, I started thawing out, but the frostbite began again when the Pastor approached me and said,

"Good evening woman of God, right this way."

He began escorting me to the pulpit. *THE PULPIT?! Oh my God! You mean, I can't sit in the congregation and just be called up when it's time for me to speak?* Every area on my body began to shake. *How am I going to speak if I cannot keep still?* As I approached the pulpit and sat down in the seating that was assigned for me, I really started panicking. *So many people! Baby Jesus, help me!* If anyone at that particular moment was paying any attention to my face, they would have known that I was yelling to myself **ABORT! ABORT!** As I continued to look throughout the congregation, I had a sudden urge to use the restroom, and, if I did not move soon, I am sure you and I both know what would have happened - major embarrassment! So, I politely asked to be shown the restroom, and I was escorted by a member of hospitality. When I reached the restroom, there was only one idea that I was pondering.

This is my chance to get out of here.

The Word of God declares that He will give you a way of escape, so I was looking for the exit sign. Surely, there was a way for me to get out of the restroom and head to the parking lot without anyone seeing me, but then I heard the soothing voice of God saying, **"Be not afraid, for I am with you."** Those words brought so much comfort to my spirit. I inhaled and exhaled, and I began to pray. I returned to the pulpit and sat down next to the Pastor. The service began a few minutes later, and there was a mighty move of God, but in my eyes, all of that changed the minute I was introduced to speak. Every bone in my body stiffened up, and my knees began to lose its stability. I was a mess. I was finally able to stand and approach the podium. As I stood there, my heart rate tripled in a matter of seconds.

My palms began to sweat.

My stomach was in knots.

I looked at my mother for support.

She smiled and nodded her head letting me know that I would be fine. "*Say something girl,*" is what I said to myself. "*Okay, okay. You've got this.*" I was trying to encourage myself, and it started working, but the problem was that no words were coming out. Everyone sat in anticipation waiting for me to say something. Finally, a word came to mind. *Hallelujah!* "Hallelujah," the congregation responded. I was shocked for some reason. They actually responded to me. Okay. Let's try this again. So, I said it again, *Hallelujah!* I received the same response from the congregation. My confidence began to build, and it started getting a little easier, and, you know what? I was able to deliver the Word that God had given me for His people.

I will never forget the title of my message — "Don't Worry, Be Happy!" Sadly though, by the time I finished the message, people did not look so happy. A horrible feeling hit the pit of my stomach. I wanted to cry. The same enthusiasm that I received during the Call and Response from the congregation before was the complete opposite of what I received while speaking. Crickets. In exception of my mother and maybe two or three others encouraging me, I could hear a pin drop. No one made a sound. All I seemed to see were eyes watching my every movement, and blank faces with no sense of engagement or interest.

Oh no! I failed! I failed God! No one liked the message! I knew that I wasn't called for this!

I strived to keep my facial expressions uplifted even though the internal part of me was broken. *I did a horrible job!* No one even came to the altar for prayer. No one. *I'm never doing this again!* In that moment, I convinced myself that I was not called, chosen or good enough and, I based it all on the responses of people. I based it all on the multitude of responses I have seen from altar calls appealed by my mother and other great men and women of God. *Why didn't I receive those types of responses?* I based it all on how I thought it should have turned out. *I knew this was a mistake!* When the service was over, something unusual started happening, at least it was unusual to me. "Thank you for that powerful Word woman of God," said one. "You blessed my soul woman of God," said another. *Wait. What?* Members and visitors began to thank me for being obedient and delivering a Rhema Word. An adult — AN ADULT — approached me, this thirteen-year-old girl, and asked me to pray for her. *Who me?* Shocked. So, I did. Following her, a youth approached me and said that she was waiting for me so that she could give her life to Christ. *Oh, my goodness! Are you serious?* She wanted me to help lead her to salvation - me. What an overwhelming feeling of joy and purpose. I felt so honored to be used as a vessel for Christ. But, after my prayer with her, I was so confused. While I was delivering the Word of God, there was hardly any response at all, but, after the service, everyone decided to tell me how well I delivered the message and was requesting prayer. Trust me, I was grateful to receive the encouragement and confirmation that I heard from the Lord, but then I began to feel a sorrow within. Why?

I was about to walk away from my purpose.

I was about to walk away from a predestined assignment.

I was about to walk away from a pivotal moment that was required for my life based on what I saw with my natural eyes, and I perceived it as failure.

Some would say that I was way too hard on myself for believing that I was not called or chosen. Yes, it was my very first experience of ministering the Gospel, so, to say that I was still "wet behind the ears" would be absolutely correct. The fact of the matter is that even at an early age, I patterned my life after those GIANTS in the gospel, such as my mother, Apostle Bobbie Jackson. In my mind, it had to look just like what I have seen in others.

I wanted to be like them. I wanted to be like my mother.

My mother never forced me into committing to a "YES" to God because she understood the level of commitment, etc. that is required. One thing she always told me, even as a little girl, was that I am a powerful vessel for God and that one-day God is going to use me mightily. She also encouraged me to be the best ME I can be for the Lord so that He can manifest His power through me even greater than He had been and still using her to this present day. (I'm taking a personal moment right now, #tears.) I had not yet grasped the concept that God could use ME on that level of greatness.

Though the ultimate outcome of the message that I delivered was a positive one and people were blessed and surrendered their lives to Christ, I still allowed what I believed to be negatives based on the lack of claps and "Hallelujahs" to affect me for months. I believed that in some way I failed God.

Now, fast forwarding back to the Forest Gump scene. Yup, I was running from the prophetic word given to me, and guess what's so funny about me running track in the opposite direction? It did not bother me at all. Do you want to know why? I was confident in singing and was becoming confident in ministering the Word of God, but prophecy is a whole different realm, and, honestly, I was not ready for it. I was so scared of accepting a call of that magnitude. Truthfully, I was still trying to process the fact that He called me to minister. Years had passed, and I was still processing the deliverance from the fear of failing God ever since that little girl ministered her first message. So, *Who me?* I did not think I was worthy of being called a Prophet.

How could I be a Prophet?

Some said that I was only following in my mother's footsteps, and that was the only reason why I was ministering. They did not believe that the Lord could use ME. It was as if I was only a shadow of my mother and not fit to carry my own oil, and I believed them. I began to believe that I was only being called and chosen by God because my mother is an amazing, powerful, and anointed woman of God. *There was no way that could ever be me*. In my mind, I automatically inherited a position of being a minister or a leader in the church just because I was a PK (Pastor's Kid). Anointed to sing, but I did not believe in myself enough to know that I could be used to that very same capacity or greater. I did not believe that I could be worthy enough to carry the weight of any mantle, let alone a prophetic one. So, I ran.

"Surely the Lord could use someone else. I'm not worthy of such an assignment." I remember when the church would have revivals and invited mighty men and women of God to impart the Word. I remember when it was standing room only. Prayer and praise would fill the atmosphere. Singing, dancing, shouting, and people running around the church as if they were on fire, but whenever a Prophet of God was there and began to operate under the unction of the Holy Ghost, people became invisible and scarce. I literally saw church members sneak out of back doors. I even saw some members slide down out of the pews so they would not be seen. Anything they could do to avoid being called out by a prophet was exactly what they did. Why? They did not want to be called out of their mess - Holiness or Hell. Back then, in the old landmark, it was not about prophesying materialistic

gains and possessions or pimping the Prophetic mantle for profit. Nowadays, whenever there is an announcement that a prophet is coming to town, sanctuaries, conferences, stadiums are filled to capacity just so they can receive "a word" from the prophet about their finances, their careers, houses, and cars, etc. "Prophets" would charge in the hundreds of dollars just to stand in a "prophetic prayer line" to receive a "word" that would not change people's lives at all but would only temporarily satisfy an itch. Truth be told, most of the time, the same word that is being spoken by the "visiting prophet" is the very same prophetic Word that has already been spoken by the Pastor, it just has not been received. Selah — (In the words of my Pastor, "I'll wait.") The Prophetic mantle is one that comes with weight, power, influence, etc. This mantle is one that could be studied repeatedly due to the depth and the revelation of the Kingdom assignment that is attached. When the prophetic Word was released to me that I was called to be a prophet to the nations, I had not yet studied in detail the realm of Prophecy. I only knew of the prophetic realm by how my mother operated and moved in the prophetic flow of the anointing of God. As a child, I was in awe and thought it was so cool to see men and women of God operating in the prophetic realm. But SEEING the flow and BEING USED to flow are two different animals. *Nope, I'm good.* It was not that I did not believe in the realm of prophecy, I just did not believe that God could use ME to fill the shoes of a prophet. Secondly, I did not believe that I can manage the pressure, the attacks, the late nights, the early mornings, and the responsibility of a prophet. *Who me? God, You chose me?* Unbelief was my state of mind. Until one night, laying in my bed, I heard my name – again – but this time it was different. I was dreaming. It was a terrifying dream that took place on the edge of a coastline, and I remember it even to this day.

Here is my dream:

Screaming and wailing filled my ears as I witnessed men, women and children running frantically trying to find shelter, trying to find a place to hide.

Wives holding their deceased husbands, husbands holding their deceased wives, children standing alone scared and crying because they cannot find their parents.

Fire resembling sharp spears shooting from the sky like comets. It was mayhem.

Suddenly, a host of heavenly angles appeared illuminating the darkness of the night as if to bring peace, but for some reason they could not come to shore. They remained in the water. Then troops appeared from the left and right marching onto the shore with weapons, and along came a demonic presence that stiffened every ounce of calm that the people were trying to hold on to. It was obvious at that time that the moment had come for people to make a decision. Live or die? Immediately I felt a boldness and strength rise up on the inside of me. I had to direct them. I had to warn them. I had to tell them. It was all up to me. I was the only one that could see the angels and the demonic presence while everyone else only saw the troops. The troops began to approach asking everyone individually whether they wanted to live for Satan and be granted the things of this world or die for the sake of Christ. Scared, many chose to live for Satan and every time someone made that decision, it was as if I was being slashed in the back with cat-o-nine-tails. One time. Two times. Three times. The pain was excruciating. When I looked up, I saw the angels standing in the water bidding people to come.

"GET TO THE WATER!" I began to scream. "THERE'S LIFE IN THE WATER! RUN! RUN TO THE WATER!"

Unfortunately, no one could hear me because my voice had been silenced. Then I began to pray under the power of the Holy Ghost. As I continued to pray, my prayer became audible so that others were able to hear me. The more I prayed the louder my voice became though the volume of my voice never increased. The prayer began to loudly echo through the atmosphere that even the troops stopped to hear, but the demonic presence began to interfere. At that very moment, with a mighty shout I screamed,

"GET TO THE WATER NOW! RUN FOR YOUR LIFE! RUN TO THE WATER!"

When the people heard, they stood in confusion and fear but, when I opened my mouth the third time, it was as if the King Himself roared through me, and people began to run towards the water. They left behind all of their earthly possessions and made the water their focus. The faster they ran, the faster the troops began to engage by hitting, punching, stabbing, and killing those that were determined. I looked up again and noticed that the angels had begun to slowly ascend yet still bidding people to come. Suddenly, I heard a trumpet blowing as if to introduce the coming of the Messiah, and then the heavens began to brighten and sparkle and twinkle light diamonds.

"DON'T LET IT BE TOO LATE! RUN! RUN TO THE WATER! THERE'S LIFE IN THE WATER!"

The angels continued to ascend yet the bidding never ceased. People continued to run. Faster. Faster they ran crying out, "PLEASE DON'T LEAVE US! WAIT! PLEASE WAIT!" Seconds later, my voiced was silenced once again and instantly the angels disappeared, and darkness covered the sky.

I woke up drenched in sweat. My respirations were through the roof, and my heart rate was untraceable. I began to cry and asked God, *"Why? Why would you allow me to see that? Why would you allow me to feel that? So much death and destruction. Why God? Why me?"* Night after night for weeks, I would experience the same exact dream over and over and over again. Though I dreamt the same dream, the way I felt about what I saw never changed. *What in the world am I supposed to do or say about this dream? Am I supposed to tell someone what I saw? Am I supposed to pray? What?* I had absolutely no clue what to do. I remembered what my mother used to always tell me, "When you don't know what to do, pray." So, I began to pray, and the Lord said, "You are My prophet."

ERRRRKKKK...bump the brakes there Lord. Umm, what did You just say? Me?

Not just a prophet, but His prophet. *A prophet, Lord?* Wheww! I did not know how to accept what He said, and so I still ran. The more I ran, the more I received prophetic dreams of different matters. God was beginning to show me different marital relationships of infidelity, the abominations that were taking place in churches, etc. OH MY GOD! The dreams and visions never stopped. Night after night, day after day, He kept showing me, speaking to me "You're my prophet." Okay, okay. I surrender. I surrender!

My "Yes" was not an easy one to submit under. Just becoming a Minister of the Gospel came with its own attacks.

But, when I gave God my "Yes" to accept the mantle of being a Prophet, there was an entirely different level of warfare that never ceases. So, when individuals come to tell me that they admire the anointing and the oil on my life and *wish* to be like me, I quickly tell them "Please don't wish to be me, because the attacks on my life you may not be able to handle. Just pray and ask God to use you according to His will for your life."

Only those who have decided to give God a *complete* Yes understand the magnitude of the warfare that comes with Kingdom assignment. Many nights I have cried because of what God shows me, tossing and turning during the night trying to forget about the visions that I have seen because they are so drastic. Waking up sometimes three or four o'clock in the morning when everyone is sleeping peacefully so that the Lord could speak to me about His children, and most importantly to show me myself and how I need to come up and operate the way He has called me. It may seem easy to others that are sitting in the congregation to see the man and woman of God in full operation under the power of the Holy Ghost. A level of awe may sweep through the room when words of prophecy are being released, and when healing and deliverance are taking place. Every time I open my mouth to sing, every time I open my mouth to pray, every time I open my mouth to speak, every time I open my mouth to prophecy or flow under the power of God, IT COMES WITH A PRICE. Servants of the Most High God are crushed and broken for the sake of the Kingdom, and it is not easy.

When the mic drops, no one sees the tears that I cry because other clergy in leadership tell me that I am not good enough to carry the mantle.

When the mic drops, no one sees the heartbreak of being called everything but a Woman of God from the lips of someone who loved and supported me in ministry once upon a time.

When the mic drops, no one sees the attacks on my life, my health, my family, and my peace of mind.

When the mic drops, no one sees the betrayal that takes place because I said "Yes" to God.

When the mic drops, no one sees the pain of having to leave behind the ones I hold dear to my heart so that they would not become collateral damage in the face of my adversity.

When the mic drops, no one sees me being stripped of my strength under the pressure and wondering why God chose me.

When Sunday is over and the mic drops, there are issues that I must face that has caused depression and even suicidal thoughts that some leaders fall victim to because of the weight. It is real, and it happens, but, even through the tears, the fear, the frustration, the doubt, the insecurity, the uncertainty, the heartbreaks, the anger, the loneliness, the abandonment, and even when I want to walk away from it all, I remember the "YES" I gave God and He wraps His arms around me and reminds me of who I am in His Word. He reassures me in the serenity of His presence that,

YES, I AM CALLED. *Even when I do not feel like I am.* **YES, I AM CHOSEN.** *Even when that little girl in me does not hear an "Amen" or a "Hallelujah,"* **YES, I AM POWERFUL.** *Even when the prayer I prayed seems voided,* **YES, I AM ANOINTED.** *Even when I am not accepted,* **YES, I AM A PROPHET OF GOD.** *Even when the prophetic word I give is not received,* **YES, I AM…***even when the mic drops.*

I pray that the following scriptures seal what I have shared with you and brings an even deeper understanding of just how chosen you are!

Hebrews 4:15 (King James Version)
"For we have not a high priest which cannot be touched with the feeling of our infirmities…"

Romans 8:30 (King James Version)

"Moreover, whom He did predestinate, them He also called: and whom He called, them He also justified: and whom He justified, them He also glorified."

Jeremiah 29:11

"For I know the thoughts that I think toward you, saith the LORD, thoughts of peace, and not of evil, to give you an expected end."

Isaiah 54:17 (King James Version)

"No weapon that is formed against thee shall prosper; and every tongue that shall rise against thee in judgment thou shalt condemn. This is the heritage of the servants of the LORD, and their righteousness is of me, saith the LORD."

Psalm 3:3

"But thou, O LORD, art a shield for me; my glory, and the lifter up of mine head."

Philippians 1:6

"Being confident of this very thing, that He which hath begun a good work in you will perform it until the day of Jesus Christ:"

There is a little song that I heard as a child that the mothers of the church used to sing that speaks the heart of a servant, and I still sing it unto the Lord this day:

> *"Jesus, use me, and oh Lord, do not refuse me, for surely there's*
> *a work that I can do! And even tho' it is humble, Lord help my will to crumble, tho' the cost will be great, I'll work for you."*

So, allow me to take this time to encourage you Man of God, allow me to speak to your heart Woman of God. I know that the cost and the Cross is great. I know that the assignment is not easy. I understand the weight that you carry but press on! **<u>Won't Stop, Can't Quit!</u>** There is work for you to do, and if God has called you and has chosen you to complete it, He has also given you the strength to bring it to pass. Manifest Man of God. Manifest Woman of God.

You can make it through even **WHEN THE MIC DROPS!**

Prayer of Strength for the Vessel

Heavenly Father,

It is in Your name that I come to you today.

I declare that You are matchless!

Your mercy is beyond my understanding!

Your love is incomprehensible!

You are holy!

You are righteous!

You are EVERYTHING!

Thank You for being my Daddy and my keeper! Thank You for choosing me as the vessel for the great work You have assigned to my life. I accept this mantle, understanding that You make no mistakes, especially when it comes to me. I say YES, knowing that no matter the depth of the call, You are with me and backing me every step of the way. I may not know the fullness of it or even how to move in it the way you have called me to, but God, I submit everything I am to learn from the greatest Teacher of all, You.

Father, it is in Your hands that I commend my life, my thoughts, my fears, concerns, and victories, too. It is in this place that I say YES and YES again! It is in this place that I repent and ask for Your forgiveness for any moment that I have reacted as if You chose the wrong one. Lord, I repent for every moment I tried to give this mantle, this charge, away. Father, I repent for every moment that delayed your manifested glory in me. Lord strip me of every insecurity and erase every doubt and fear. Teach my hands to war and my fingers to fight! Lord, I am willing. Lord I am ready.

I am ready to be used by You.

In Jesus' name, Amen.

Are you ready to begin your literary journey?

Contact us today!

Fiery Beacon Publishing House, LLC

1400 Battleground Avenue, Suite 214B

Greensboro, North Carolina

27408

Phone: 336.285.5794

Email: fbphinfo@fierybeaconpublishinghousellc.com

Website: www.fierybeaconpublishinghousellc.com

Let's Ignite Your *Literary* Genius!

www.ingramcontent.com/pod-product-compliance
Lightning Source LLC
Chambersburg PA
CBHW070505100426
42743CB00010B/1762